Hamilton Beach Bread Machine Cookbook

120 Classic, Tasty, No-Fuss Recipes for Your Daily Cravings
with Your Hamilton Beach Bread Machine

Alicia R. Tuttle

Copyright© 2020 By Alicia R. Tuttle All Rights Reserved

This book is copyright protected. It is only for personal use. You cannot amend, distribute, sell, use, quote or paraphrase any part of the content within this book, without the consent of the author or publisher.

Under no circumstances will any blame or legal responsibility be held against the publisher, or author, for any damages, reparation, or monetary loss due to the information contained within this book, either directly or indirectly.

Disclaimer Notice:

Please note the information contained within this document is for educational and entertainment purposes only. All effort has been executed to present accurate, up to date, reliable, complete information. No warranties of any kind are declared or implied. Readers acknowledge that the author is not engaged in the rendering of legal, financial, medical or professional advice. The content within this book has been derived from various sources. Please consult a licensed professional before attempting any techniques outlined in this book.

By reading this document, the reader agrees that under no circumstances is the author responsible for any losses, direct or indirect, that are incurred as a result of the use of the information contained within this document, including, but not limited to, errors, omissions, or inaccuracies.

Content

1　*Introduction*

2　*Chapter 1* The Basics of Hamilton Beach Bread Machine

9　*Chapter 2* Whole Wheat Breads

21　*Chapter 3* Fruit and Vegetable Breads

33　*Chapter 4* Spice and Herb Breads

48　*Chapter 5* Sweet Breads

60　*Chapter 6* Sourdough Breads

70　*Chapter 7* Nut and Seed Breads

80　*Chapter 8* Specialty Breads

89　*Appendix 1* Measurement Conversion Chart
90　*Appendix 2* Recipe Index

Introduction

Cooking is my passion and a favorite hobby ever since I was young. I have been experimenting with new recipes and serving food to my family and friends whenever a recipe is ready. Most of the time, the feedback was very encouraging, which has enhanced my confidence and boosted my morale to believe in my skill. Thus, I chose to make a career out of it by writing and compiling recipe books. I wrote every successful tasty recipe that I have tried and compiled it into a cookbook. It has been the right thing I have done, and I am so happy to share it with you.

Hamilton Beach Bread Machine was such a choice for me; the brand is reliable and reputed. For years it has been serving the kitchens and received many accolades from food specialists. For the same reason, I bought the machine, and it has some great features and functions that make it the favorite of all. The company also offers a bread-making recipe book to make your bread making a happy experience along with the Hamilton Beach Bread Machine.

This book I have written from my personal experience. It is a compilation of 120 bread recipes that any food lovers would love to experiment with and serve your dear ones as well.

It doesn't matter if you are a first-time cook or using the appliance for the first time; I have tried my best effort to guide you properly in making homely bread and other items with the bread machine in the cookbook. I have added the ingredients required for the recipes, quantity, cooking time, and detailed description you need to know to make the bread and other foods. But before going directly to the recipes, get to know about the machine.

Chapter 1
The Basics of Hamilton Beach Bread Machine

12 Program Settings or Cycles

   Hamilton Beach Bread Machine comes with 12 different settings. The settings are basic, French, sweet, quick, gluten-free, and 1.5-pound express, 2-pound express, dough, jam, cake, whole grain, and bake. The control panel on the top lid includes cycle, crust, loaf size, delay timer, start/stop button. You can set the crust to light, medium or dark. Remove the bread as soon as the baking is over to avoid getting it darker. With the 12-setting, the bread-making is comfortable like a breeze.

1. Basic program

The basic program is for making mixed and white bread using the basic bread flour. White bread is rich in calcium, and it is best to maintain healthy bones and teeth. Mixed bread has more fiber and has more nutritional values.

2. French program

With the French feature, you can make bread with refined flour. Bread made of fine flour will be crispier and fluffier in appearance. Its chewable structure makes it different from ordinary white bread. It has more vitamin B, zinc, and iron. Hence, it is more beneficial from a health point of view. Since it is not from whole grain flour, it will have a low amount of fiber and more carbs.

3. Sweet program

It is a perfect option for making sweet bread by adding grated coconut, fruit juices, sugar, dry fruits, raisins, etc. The rising period will be more than the white bread, and because of this long raising, the bread will be airy and lightweight.

4. Quick program

With the quick program, you can knead the flour within a short period of the time required for making a basic bread. This program is suitable for making bread without adding yeast.

5. Gluten-Free program

The Hamilton Beach Bread Machine comes with a gluten-free program, ideal for making gluten-free mixes and bread. Gluten-free bread is an inevitable food for people undergoing a weight loss regime. The primary benefit of gluten-free foods is that it can increase energy levels and maintain weight loss. The gluten-free diet is essential for managing celiac diseases and other treatments related to gluten in medical terms.

6. 1.5-pound Express program

Within 58 minutes, by adding quick-rising yeast, you can bake a 1.5-pound loaf of bread. During the process, the bread machine will take care of the kneading, rising, and baking. By comparing to the basic cycle program, the bread loaf will be small and rough.

7. 2-pound Express

With this program, you can bake a 2-pound loaf of bread within 58 minutes by adding the required amount of quick-rising yeast.

8. Dough program

The program is simple to use for making dough for pizza, buns, etc. During the program, no baking happens, and you can use the kneaded dough in a conventional oven.

9. Jam program

When you want to make fresh homemade jams, go for the option available with Hamilton Beach Bread Machine. It is one of the best choices you can find in the bread machine, which is highly beneficial for making homely jams.

10. Cake program

In this feature, besides kneading the flour and rising, the bread machine bakes the cake as per the present options. You need to add baking powder or food-grade soda to make a perfect cake for the rising.

11. Whole Grain Bread program

The Whole Grain program is ideal when you want to bake bread with whole wheat flour. The program has the features to meet the kneading requirement and rising of the flour to get a perfectly baked heavy bread.

12. Bake program

You can use this option if you want to bake a poorly baked bread. The program won't have features of rising and kneading.

The Benefits of Hamilton Beach Bread Machine

- **Spacious Interior**—Hamilton Beach Bread Machine has a very spacious interior. It is possible to bake bread for a whole week with the appliance in a single-use. The maximum time you need to spend is 2 to 3 hours a day in a week. You can even bake a whole dough of 1.5 or 2 pounds in this appliance. The bread baking paddle is spacious and removable as well, which makes your job easier.

- **Easy to Use Bread Machine**—The whole process of bread making is easy with Hamilton Beach Bread Machine. You need to add the necessary ingredients as per the given order. Add the liquid ingredient first into the bread pan, then salt or sugar, then the flour, and finally yeast. Choose a cycle you want to prepare from the 12 settings and press the start button on the top. It is not tough to use the machine, and with the help of the manual, you can use it more easily.

- **Clear Display Screen**—The display screen plays a vital role in providing the cooking status and making cooking settings. The bread machine comes with a display screen on the top portion of the cooker, which is clear enough to read while the bread cooking is in progress. Everything you set in the machine would show there on the screen.

- **Non-Sticky Bread Pan**—Maintenance of Hamilton Beach Bread Machine is easy. The bread pan comes with sturdy non-sticky material and is removable. Therefore, you wouldn't face any trouble to clean or to release the bread after baking. Cleaning is a challenging task than cooking for most of us, but with the Hamilton Beach Bread Machine, it wouldn't be an issue at all.

- **Satisfied Performance**—My experience with the machine is extremely satisfactory, and I am content with its performance. It seldom breaks down during the process, and I can say that it has low maintenance. Apart from the bread-making features, I recommend the bread machine to my readers because of its low maintenance.

We can even see the term gluten-free labeled in bread making machines, but most of them won't bring the results as they claim. I haven't found such an issue in Hamilton's beach bread machine because it provided me with the desired results.

- **Value for Money**—Even if you spend a little extra amount for the bread machine than the average bread machine, it is worth paying considering the quality and performance it offers. The machine is a little heavy, you can also hear some gentle noises (not louder) while kneading the dough, but it is not even an issue at all comparing its benefits.

Some Notable Features

- Versatility
- Durability
- Low noise
- Delayed timer
- Easy to use
- Easy cleaning
- 12 different cycles
- 2-Lb bread machine
- Weight 11.86 pounds
- Low maintenance
- 3 crust settings
- Holes for ventilation on the top lid
- More than 4 stars rated
- Non-slip feet
- Cool touch body
- One-year warranty
- Recipe book by Hamilton

Parts and Accessories

- Viewing glass window
- Big display
- Non-sticky bread pan
- Two kneading paddles
- Tool for removing the paddle
- Control panel
- Ventilation hole on the top lid
- Baking chamber
- Measure spoon
- Measuring bowl

Let's Try the Bread Recipes

The bread that we can get from the groceries is mostly with processed ingredients. So, it is not healthy food. When you can make bread at home, the ingredients you use are not processed. That makes a lot of difference from depending on the groceries, and I strongly recommend using Hamilton Breach Bread Machine for making the bread at home.

The bread-making won't consume much of your time because it takes only 5-10 minutes to add the ingredients into the bread pan. After that, choose the cycle buttons, the machine will do the rest for you.

With Hamilton Beach Bread Machine, forget about the boring breakfast. I have included various delicious recipes in my cookbook, which you can try quickly at your home. Try my unique 120 bread recipes and have fun in quality bread making and baking. You must wonder by seeing its features. Even for baking bread, it has got so many varieties, and it will always surprise you.

Chapter 2

Whole Wheat Breads

11	Basic Whole Wheat Bread
11	Whole Wheat Honey Bread
12	Whole Wheat Sesame Bread
12	Toasted Sesame Seed Whole Wheat Bread
13	Super Seed Whole Wheat Bread
13	Pure Whole Wheat Bread
14	Ranch Wheat Bran Whole Wheat Bread
14	Buttermilk Spelt Bread
15	Maple Whole Wheat White Bread
15	Balsamic and Sour Cream Rye Bread
16	Orange Rye Bread
16	Dutch Dark Rye Bread
17	Caraway Rye Bread
17	Beer Rye Whole Wheat Bread
18	Pumpernickel Bread
18	Limpa Bread
19	Pumpkin Paximadia
20	Cracked Rye Sesame Bread

Basic Whole Wheat Bread

Makes 2 pounds loaf

- 1 1/3 cups water
- 1 large egg
- 2½ tablespoons vegetable or nut oil
- 3¼ cups bread flour
- ¾ cup whole wheat flour
- 4 tablespoons dry buttermilk powder
- 2½ tablespoons dark brown sugar
- 1 tablespoon plus 1 teaspoon gluten
- 2 teaspoons salt
- 2½ teaspoons SAF yeast or 1 tablespoon bread machine yeast

1. Place all the ingredients in the pan according to the order in the manufacturer's instructions. Set crust on medium or dark and program for the Basic cycle; press Start. The dough ball will be moist.
2. When the baking cycle ends, immediately remove the bread from the pan and place it on a rack. Let cool to room temperature before slicing.

Whole Wheat Honey Bread

Makes 2 pounds loaf

- ½ cup water
- 2/3 cup milk
- 1/3 cup honey
- 1 large egg
- 1½ tablespoons butter, cut into pieces
- 2 2/3 cups bread flour
- 1 1/3 cups whole wheat flour
- 1 tablespoon plus 2 teaspoons gluten
- 2½ teaspoons salt
- 1 tablespoon SAF yeast or 1 tablespoon plus ½ teaspoon bread machine yeast

1. Place all the ingredients in the pan according to the order in the manufacturer's instructions. Set crust on medium and program for the Basic cycle; press Start.
2. When the baking cycle ends, immediately remove the bread from the pan and place it on a rack. Let cool to room temperature before slicing.

Whole Wheat Sesame Bread

Makes 2 pounds loaf

- ¾ cup water
- ¾ cup milk
- 3 tablespoons butter, cut into pieces
- 3 cups bread flour
- 1 cup whole wheat flour
- 3 tablespoons light or dark brown sugar
- 1 tablespoon plus 2 teaspoons sesame seeds
- 1 tablespoon plus 2 teaspoons gluten
- 2 teaspoons salt
- 2¼ teaspoons SAF yeast or 2¾ teaspoons bread machine yeast

1. Place all the ingredients in the pan according to the order in the manufacturer's instructions. Set crust on medium and program for the Basic cycle; press Start.
2. When the baking cycle ends, immediately remove the bread from the pan and place it on a rack. Let cool to room temperature before slicing.

Toasted Sesame Seed Whole Wheat Bread

Makes 2 pounds loaf

- 2½ tablespoons sesame seeds
- 1²⁄₃ cups water
- 3 tablespoons honey
- ¼ cup sesame oil
- 4½ cups whole wheat flour
- 3 tablespoons gluten
- 2¼ teaspoons sea salt
- 1 tablespoon SAF yeast or 1 tablespoon plus ½ teaspoon bread machine yeast

1. Place the sesame seeds in a dry skillet. Cook over medium heat, shaking constantly, until the seeds are lightly toasted, about 2 minutes. Set aside to cool.
2. Place all the ingredients in the pan according to the order in the manufacturer's instructions. Set crust on medium and program for the Whole Grain cycle; press Start.
3. When the baking cycle ends, immediately remove the bread from the pan and place it on a rack. Let cool to room temperature before slicing.

Super Seed Whole Wheat Bread

Makes 2 pounds loaf

- 1 2/3 cups water
- 3 tablespoons sunflower seed oil
- 2 cups bread flour
- 2 cups whole wheat flour
- ¼ cup nonfat dry milk
- 3 tablespoons brown sugar
- 1 tablespoon plus 1 teaspoon gluten
- 1½ teaspoons salt
- 2½ teaspoons SAF yeast or 1 tablespoon bread machine yeast
- ½ cup raw sunflower seeds
- 2½ tablespoons sesame seeds
- 2½ teaspoons poppy seeds

1. Place the ingredients, except the seeds, in the pan according to the order in the manufacturer's instructions. Set crust on medium and program for the Basic or Whole Grain cycle; press Start. When the machine beeps, or between Knead 1 and Knead 2, add all the seeds.
2. When the baking cycle ends, immediately remove the bread from the pan and place it on a rack. Let cool to room temperature before slicing.

Pure Whole Wheat Bread

Makes 2 pounds loaf

- 1 cup water
- 1 cup milk
- 3 tablespoons canola oil
- 1/3 cup light molasses
- 5 cups whole wheat flour
- ¼ cup gluten
- 2¼ teaspoons salt
- 1 tablespoon plus ½ teaspoon SAF yeast or 1 tablespoon plus 1 teaspoon bread machine yeast

1. Place all the ingredients in the pan according to the order in the manufacturer's instructions. Set crust on medium and program for the Whole Grain cycle; press Start.
2. When the baking cycle ends, immediately remove the bread from the pan and place it on a rack. Let cool to room temperature before slicing.

Ranch Wheat Bran Whole Wheat Bread

Makes 2 pounds loaf

- 1¾ cups water
- ¼ cup canola oil
- 3 tablespoons honey
- 3 tablespoons molasses
- 4½ cups whole wheat flour
- ½ cup wheat bran
- 3½ tablespoons gluten
- 1 tablespoon plus 1 teaspoon poppy seeds
- 2 teaspoons salt
- 1 tablespoon plus ½ teaspoon SAF yeast or 1 tablespoon plus 1 teaspoon bread machine yeast

1. Place all the ingredients in the pan according to the order in the manufacturer's instructions. Set crust on dark and program for the Whole Grain cycle; press Start. After 10 minutes, check the dough ball with your finger. It will be sticky. Add 1 to 2 tablespoons more flour. The dough will still be very sticky; don't worry, it will absorb the liquid during the rises. If you add too much flour, the bread will be dense, rather than springy. If you don't add the extra flour as needed, the top can collapse.
2. When the baking cycle ends, immediately remove the bread from the pan and place it on a rack. Let cool to room temperature before slicing.

Buttermilk Spelt Bread

Makes 2 pounds loaf

- ½ cup water
- ¾ cup buttermilk
- 2 tablespoons canola oil
- 1 tablespoon whipped reduced-fat margarine
- 3 cups whole grain spelt flour
- 1 cup bread flour
- 3 tablespoons dark brown sugar
- 1 tablespoon plus 2 teaspoons gluten
- 2 teaspoons salt
- 2¼ teaspoons SAF yeast or 2¾ teaspoons bread machine yeast

1. Place all the ingredients in the pan according to the order in the manufacturer's instructions. Set crust on dark and program for the Whole Grain cycle; press Start. The dough ball will look sticky. Do not add too much flour, the dough will smooth out.
2. When the baking cycle ends, immediately remove the bread from the pan and place it on a rack. Let cool to room temperature before slicing.

Maple Whole Wheat White Bread

Makes 2 pounds loaf

- 1½ cups water
- 3 tablespoons nut oil or olive oil
- ⅓ cup maple syrup
- 4⅓ cups white whole wheat flour
- 1½ tablespoons gluten
- 2 teaspoons salt
- 2½ teaspoons SAF yeast or 1 tablespoon bread machine yeast

1. Place all the ingredients in the pan according to the order in the manufacturer's instructions. Set crust on dark and program for the Basic or Whole Grain cycle; press Start.
2. When the baking cycle ends, immediately remove the bread from the pan and place it on a rack. Let cool to room temperature before slicing.

Balsamic and Sour Cream Rye Bread

Makes 2 pounds loaf

- ¾ cup water
- 2½ tablespoons balsamic vinegar
- 1 cup sour cream
- 3 tablespoons dark honey or molasses
- 3 tablespoons vegetable oil
- 2½ cups bread flour
- 1½ cups dark rye flour
- 1½ tablespoons instant potato flakes
- 1 tablespoon plus 2 teaspoons gluten
- 1 tablespoon plus 1 teaspoon caraway seeds
- 1½ teaspoons ground coriander seeds
- 2 teaspoons salt
- 2½ teaspoons SAF yeast or 1 tablespoon bread machine yeast

1. Place all the ingredients in the pan according to the order in the manufacturer's instructions. Set crust on medium and program for the Basic or Whole Grain cycle; press Start. The dough ball will be well shaped, but tacky and spread like a puddle during the risings.
2. When the baking cycle ends, immediately remove the bread from the pan and carefully place it on a rack. Let cool to room temperature before slicing.

Orange Rye Bread

Makes 2 pounds loaf

- 1½ cups water
- ¼ cup honey
- 3 tablespoons vegetable oil
- 2¾ cups bread flour
- 1¾ cups medium rye flour
- 1 tablespoon plus 2 teaspoons gluten
- 1 tablespoon fennel seeds
- 2 teaspoons grated orange zest or dried orange peel
- 1½ teaspoons salt
- 2½ teaspoons SAF yeast or 1 tablespoon bread machine yeast

1. Place all the ingredients in the pan according to the order in the manufacturer's instructions. Set crust on medium and program for the Basic cycle; press Start.
2. When the baking cycle ends, immediately remove the bread from the pan and place it on a rack. Let cool to room temperature before slicing.

Dutch Dark Rye Bread

Makes 2 pounds loaf

- 1½ cups water
- 4 tablespoons butter, melted
- 2 tablespoons molasses
- 2⅓ cups bread flour
- 1⅓ cup medium or dark rye flour
- ⅓ cup wheat bran
- 3 tablespoons unsweetened Dutch-process cocoa powder
- 1 tablespoon plus 1 teaspoon gluten
- 2 teaspoons instant espresso powder
- 2 teaspoons caraway seeds
- ¾ teaspoon fennel seeds
- 2 teaspoons salt
- 2½ teaspoons SAF yeast or 1 tablespoon bread machine yeast

1. Place all the ingredients in the pan according to the order in the manufacturer's instructions. Set crust on medium and program for the Basic or Whole Grain cycle; press Start.
2. When the baking cycle ends, immediately remove the bread from the pan and place it on a rack. Let cool to room temperature before slicing.

Caraway Rye Bread

Makes 2 pounds loaf

- 1½ cups water
- 2 tablespoons canola oil
- 2½ cups bread flour
- 1½ cups medium rye flour
- 3 tablespoons brown sugar
- 1 tablespoon plus 2 teaspoons gluten
- 2 tablespoons caraway seeds
- 2 teaspoons salt
- 1 tablespoon SAF yeast or 1 tablespoon plus ½ teaspoon bread machine yeast

1. Place all the ingredients in the pan according to the order in the manufacturer's instructions. Set crust on medium and program for the Basic cycle; press Start. The dough ball will be soft and springy.
2. When the baking cycle ends, immediately remove the bread from the pan and place it on a rack. Let cool to room temperature before slicing.

Beer Rye Whole Wheat Bread

Makes 2 pounds loaf

- 1⅓ cups beer
- ¼ cup apple cider vinegar
- 3 tablespoons honey
- 2 tablespoons butter, melted
- 1½ tablespoons minced raw shallot
- 2½ cups bread flour
- 1 cup light or medium rye flour
- ½ cup whole wheat flour
- 3 tablespoons yellow cornmeal
- 2½ tablespoons gluten
- 2½ teaspoons caraway seeds
- 2 teaspoons salt
- 1 tablespoon plus 1 teaspoon SAF yeast or 1 tablespoon plus 1½ teaspoons bread machine yeast

1. Open the container of beer and let stand at room temperature for a few hours to go flat.
2. Place all the ingredients in the pan according to the order in the manufacturer's instructions. Set crust on medium and program for the Basic cycle; press Start.
3. When the baking cycle ends, immediately remove the bread from the pan and place it on a rack. Let cool to room temperature before slicing.

Pumpernickel Bread

Makes 2 pounds loaf

- 1 2/3 cups water
- 4½ tablespoons molasses
- 3 tablespoons butter, melted
- 2 cups bread flour
- 1 1/3 cups medium or dark rye flour
- 2/3 cup whole wheat flour
- 1/3 cup cornmeal
- ¼ cup unsweetened Dutch-process cocoa powder
- 2½ tablespoons brown sugar
- 2 tablespoons nonfat dry milk
- 2 tablespoons gluten
- ¾ teaspoon instant espresso powder
- 1 tablespoon caraway seeds
- 2 teaspoons salt
- 1 tablespoon SAF yeast or 1 tablespoon plus ½ teaspoon bread machine yeast
- ½ cup raw sunflower seeds

1. Place the ingredients, except the sunflower seeds, in the pan according to the order in the manufacturer's instructions. Set crust on medium and program for the Basic or Whole Grain cycle; press Start. When the machine beeps, or between Knead 1 and Knead 2, add the sunflower seeds.
2. When the baking cycle ends, immediately remove the bread from the pan and place it on a rack. Let cool to room temperature before slicing.

Limpa Bread

Makes 2 pounds loaf

- 1 cup water
- ½ cup milk
- 2 tablespoons molasses
- 2 tablespoons brown sugar
- 3 tablespoons butter, cut into pieces
- 2½ cups bread flour
- 1½ cups medium rye flour
- 1 tablespoon plus 1 teaspoon gluten
- ¾ teaspoon fennel seeds, crushed
- ¾ teaspoon aniseed, crushed
- 2 teaspoons grated orange zest
- 1¾ teaspoons salt
- 2¼ teaspoons SAF yeast or 2¾ teaspoons bread machine yeast

1. Place all the ingredients in the pan according to the order in the manufacturer's instructions. Set crust on medium and program for the Basic cycle; press Start.
2. When the baking cycle ends, immediately remove the bread from the pan and place it on a rack. Let cool to room temperature before slicing.

Pumpkin Paximadia

Makes 10 pieces paximadia

- 1¼ cups water
- 2 tablespoons olive oil
- 2 tablespoons honey
- 2½ cups whole wheat flour
- 1 cup bread flour
- 1 teaspoon pumpkin pie spice blend, or ½ teaspoon each ground cinnamon and cloves
- 1 teaspoon salt
- 2 teaspoons SAF yeast or 2½ teaspoons bread machine yeast

1. Place all the ingredients in the bread pan according to the order in the manufacturer's instructions. Program for the Dough cycle; press Start. The dough ball will be firm, yet springy and moist.
2. Line a baking sheet with parchment paper. Turn the dough out onto a clean work surface. Knead to form a oblong oval loaf 11 by 4 inches. Place, seam side down, on the baking sheet. Using a serrated knife, carefully cut the loaf all the way through with a gentle back and forth sawing motion, into 1- to 1¼-inch slices to make 10 slices. After cutting all the pieces, place one hand on each end of the loaf and gently press together to make a whole loaf with separations that you can see clearly. Cover loosely with plastic wrap. Let rest at room temperature for 20 minutes.
3. Meanwhile, preheat the oven to 350ºF (180ºC).
4. Bake for 35 to 40 minutes, or until deep brown and the bottom sounds hollow when tapped with your finger. Remove the bread from the oven and transfer the loaf to a rack to cool. Leave the parchment on the baking sheet; you will use it again.
5. When the loaf is completely cooled, at least 2 hours, separate the slices by tearing them apart with your hands, the way it is done in Greece. Set the oven at its lowest setting, about 200ºF (93ºC). Place the slices on their flat sides on the parchment-lined baking sheet. Place in the oven and let the toasts dry out slowly, about 5 hours. Remove from the oven and cool completely. Store in an airtight tin.

Cracked Rye Sesame Bread

Makes 2 pounds loaf

- 1¾ cups boiling water
- ⅔ cup cracked rye
- ¼ cup dark brown sugar
- 4 tablespoons butter
- 1½ teaspoons salt
- 2¼ cups bread flour
- 1⅓ cups medium rye flour
- ½ cup nonfat dry milk
- 1 tablespoon plus 2 teaspoons gluten
- 1½ tablespoons sesame seeds
- 1½ tablespoons wheat germ
- 1 tablespoon SAF yeast or 1 tablespoon plus ½ teaspoon bread machine yeast

1. Pour the boiling water over the cracked rye in a bowl. Add the brown sugar, butter, and salt. Let stand 1 hour on the counter to soften.
2. Place the ingredients in the pan according to the order in the manufacturer's instructions, adding the grain and its soaking liquid as the liquid ingredients. Set crust on medium and program for the Basic or Whole Grain cycle; press Start.
3. When the baking cycle ends, immediately remove the bread from the pan and place it on a rack. Let cool to room temperature before slicing.

Chapter 3

Fruit and Vegetable Breads

23	Honey Black Olive Rye Bread
23	Garlic Butter Bread
24	Sun-Dried Tomato Whole Wheat Bread
24	Sweet Potato Bread with Cranberry
25	Zucchini Whole Wheat Bread
25	Wheat Berry Bread with Cherries
26	Cinnamon Prune Whole Wheat Bread
26	Crystallized Ginger Carrot Bread
27	Apple Bread
27	Banana Bread with Walnut
28	Herb and Walnut Bread
28	Parsley Corn Bread
29	Balsamic Onion Rye Bread
29	Chive and Parsley Pull-Apart Rolls
30	Prosciutto Bread
31	Winter Squash Cloverleaf Rolls
32	Cinnamon Date Walnut Swirl Bread

Honey Black Olive Rye Bread

Makes 2 pounds loaf

- 1 1/3 cups fat-free milk
- 1/3 cup olive oil
- 1½ tablespoons honey
- 3¼ cups bread flour
- ¾ cup rye flour
- 1 tablespoon plus 2 teaspoons gluten
- ¾ teaspoon salt
- 2½ teaspoons SAF yeast or 1 tablespoon bread machine yeast
- 1¼ full cups pitted black olive pieces

1. Place the ingredients, except the olives, in the pan according to the order in the manufacturer's instructions. Set crust on medium and program for the French cycle; press Start. The dough ball will be slightly sticky. Halfway through Knead 2, open the machine and add the olives. If you like big chunks of olives, press Pause at the beginning of Rise 1 instead, remove the dough, pat it into a rectangle, and sprinkle with the olives. Roll up the dough and gently knead a few times to distribute the olives. Return the dough ball to the machine and press Start to resume the rising.
2. When the baking cycle ends, immediately remove the bread from the pan and place it on a rack. Let cool to room temperature before slicing.

Garlic Butter Bread

Makes 2 pounds loaf

- 4 cloves garlic
- 3 tablespoons unsalted butter, softened
- 1½ cups water
- 4 cups bread flour
- 1 tablespoon plus 1 teaspoon gluten
- 1½ tablespoons sugar
- 1¾ teaspoons salt
- 2½ teaspoons SAF yeast or 1 tablespoon bread machine yeast

1. Peel the garlic cloves and press into the butter. Mash together.
2. Place all the ingredients in the pan according to the order in the manufacturer's instructions. Add the garlic butter with the liquid ingredients. Set crust on medium and program for French cycle; press Start.
3. When the baking cycle ends, immediately remove the bread from the pan and place it on a rack. Let cool to room temperature before slicing.

Sun-Dried Tomato Whole Wheat Bread

Makes 2 pounds loaf

- 1½ cups water
- ¼ cup tomato paste
- ½ cup chopped oil-packed sun-dried tomatoes, with their oil
- 3⅔ cups bread flour
- ⅔ cup whole wheat flour
- 2 tablespoons gluten
- 2 teaspoons salt
- 2¼ teaspoons SAF yeast or 2¾ teaspoons bread machine yeast

1. Place all the ingredients in the pan according to the order in the manufacturer's instructions. Set crust on medium or dark and program for the Basic cycle; press Start.
2. When the baking cycle ends, immediately remove the bread from the pan and place it on a rack. Let cool to room temperature before slicing.

Sweet Potato Bread with Cranberry

Makes 2 pounds loaf

- ⅔ cup fat-free milk
- 1 cup puréed sweet potatoes
- ¼ cup sour cream
- 4 cups bread flour
- 1 tablespoon plus 1 teaspoon gluten
- 2 teaspoons salt
- Grated zest of 1 orange
- 2½ teaspoons SAF yeast or 1 tablespoon bread machine yeast
- 1 cup fresh whole cranberries

1. Place the ingredients, except the cranberries, in the pan according to the order in the manufacturer's instructions. Set crust on medium and program for the Basic cycle; press Start. When the machine beeps, or between Knead 1 and Knead 2, add the cranberries; they will break up some with the action of the blade.
2. When the baking cycle ends, immediately remove the bread from the pan and place it on a rack. Let cool to room temperature before slicing.

Zucchini Whole Wheat Bread

Makes 2 pounds loaf

- 1 cup fat-free milk
- 1½ cups shredded zucchini
- 3 tablespoons olive oil
- 2⅔ cups bread flour
- 1⅓ cups whole wheat flour
- 2 tablespoons dark brown sugar
- Grated zest of 1 lemon
- 1 tablespoon plus 1 teaspoon gluten
- 2 teaspoons salt
- 2¼ teaspoons SAF yeast or 2¾ teaspoons bread machine yeast

1. Place all the ingredients in the pan according to the order in the manufacturer's instructions. Set crust on medium and program for the Basic cycle; press Start.
2. When the baking cycle ends, immediately remove the bread from the pan and place it on a rack. Let cool to room temperature before slicing.

Wheat Berry Bread with Cherries

Makes 2 pounds loaf

- ½ cup wheat berries
- 1 cup water
- 1¼ cups water
- 1 large egg white
- 3 tablespoons canola oil
- ⅓ cup honey
- 4 cups bread flour
- 1 tablespoon gluten
- 2 teaspoons salt
- 1 tablespoon SAF yeast or 1 tablespoon plus ½ teaspoon bread machine yeast
- ⅔ cup tart dried cherries tossed with 1 tablespoon flour

1. Combine the wheat berries and the 1 cup of water in a saucepan. Bring to a boil. Reduce the heat, partially cover, and simmer for about 45 minutes, until chewy and tender. Drain off the excess water and let cool to warm.
2. Place the ingredients, except the wheat berries and the cherries, in the pan according to the order in the manufacturer's instructions. Set crust on dark and program for the Basic cycle; press Start. When the machine beeps, or at the pause between Knead 1 and 2, add the wheat berries and the cherries. The dough ball will be quite soft and nubby.
3. When the baking cycle ends, immediately remove the bread from the pan and place it on a rack. Let cool to room temperature before slicing.

Cinnamon Prune Whole Wheat Bread

Makes 2 pounds loaf

- 1½ cups water
- 4 tablespoons unsalted butter, cut into pieces
- 2¾ cups bread flour
- 1¼ cups whole wheat flour
- 3 tablespoons light brown sugar
- 1 tablespoon plus 1 teaspoon gluten
- 1¾ teaspoons salt
- 1¼ teaspoons ground cinnamon
- ⅓ teaspoon fresh-ground nutmeg
- 2½ teaspoons SAF yeast or 1 tablespoon bread machine yeast
- 12 pitted prunes (about 4 ounces / 113 g), chopped

1. Place the ingredients, except the prunes, in the pan according to the order in the manufacturer's instructions. Set crust on dark and program for the Basic cycle; press Start. When the machine beeps, or between Knead 1 and Knead 2, add the prunes. If you like big chunks of prunes, press Pause at the beginning of Rise 1, remove the dough, pat it into a rectangle, and sprinkle with the prunes. Roll up the dough and gently knead it a few times to distribute the prunes. Return the dough ball to the machine and press Start to resume the rising.
2. When the baking cycle ends, immediately remove the bread from the pan and place it on a rack. Let cool to room temperature before slicing.

Crystallized Ginger Carrot Bread

Makes 2 pounds loaf

- ¼ cup fat-free milk
- 1 (6-ounce / 170-g) jar junior baby food strained carrots or ¾ cup puréed carrots
- 2 large eggs
- 3 tablespoons unsalted butter, cut into pieces
- 4 cups bread flour
- ⅓ cup chopped crystallized ginger
- 1 tablespoon plus 1 teaspoon gluten
- 2 teaspoons salt
- 2 teaspoons SAF yeast or 2½ teaspoons bread machine yeast

1. Place all the ingredients in the pan according to the order in the manufacturer's instructions. Set crust on dark and program for the Basic cycle; press Start.
2. When the baking cycle ends, immediately remove the bread from the pan and place it on a rack. Let cool to room temperature before slicing.

Apple Bread

Makes 2 pounds loaf

- ½ cup apple juice
- ¾ cup unsweetened applesauce
- 1 large egg
- 3 tablespoons unsalted butter, cut into pieces
- 4 cups bread flour
- ¼ cup light brown sugar, optional
- 1 tablespoon plus 1 teaspoon gluten
- 2 teaspoons salt
- 1¼ teaspoons ground cinnamon or apple pie spice
- ½ teaspoon baking soda
- 2¼ teaspoons SAF yeast or 2¾ teaspoons bread machine yeast

1. Place all the ingredients in the pan according to the order in the manufacturer's instructions. Set crust on medium and program for the Basic or Sweet cycle; press Start.
2. When the baking cycle ends, immediately remove the bread from the pan and place it on a rack. Let cool to room temperature before slicing.

Banana Bread with Walnut

Serves 12

- 3 large, overripe bananas
- 8 tablespoons sugar
- 2 eggs
- 2 cups flour, sifted
- 1 teaspoon salt
- 1 teaspoon baking powder
- ½ teaspoon vanilla extract
- 1 teaspoon cinnamon
- 2 tablespoons walnuts, chopped
- Butter, for greasing pan

1. Mash the bananas with a fork and add the sugar in a large mixing bowl until smooth.
2. Butter the bread maker loaf pan; pour in the banana mixture.
3. Add the eggs, flour, and remaining dry ingredients.
4. Select Sweet cycle, medium crust color, and press Start.
5. Transfer to a cooling rack for 15 minutes before slicing to serve.

Herb and Walnut Bread

Makes 2 pounds loaf

- 1½ cups plus 1 tablespoon water
- 2 tablespoons walnut oil
- 4 cups bread flour
- 1½ tablespoons light brown sugar
- ¾ cup mixed fresh herbs, minced
- ⅓ cup walnuts
- 1 tablespoon plus 1 teaspoon gluten
- 2 teaspoons salt
- 2½ teaspoons SAF yeast or 1 tablespoon bread machine yeast

1. Place all the ingredients in the pan according to the order in the manufacturer's instructions. Set crust on dark and program for the Basic cycle; press Start.
2. When the baking cycle ends, immediately remove the bread from the pan and place it on a rack. Let cool to room temperature before slicing.

Parsley Corn Bread

Makes 2 pounds loaf

- 1 (11-ounce / 312-g) can of corn with liquid
- ⅓ cup buttermilk
- 3 tablespoons canola or olive oil
- 3 tablespoons honey
- 2¾ cups bread flour
- 1¼ cups yellow cornmeal
- ⅓ cup minced fresh parsley
- 1¾ tablespoons poultry seasoning
- ¾ teaspoon garlic powder
- 1 tablespoon plus 2 teaspoons gluten
- 1½ teaspoons salt
- 2½ teaspoons SAF yeast or 1 tablespoon bread machine yeast

1. Place all the ingredients in the pan according to the order in the manufacturer's instructions. Set crust on dark and program for the Basic cycle; press Start.
2. When the baking cycle ends, immediately remove the bread from the pan and place it on a rack. Let cool to room temperature before slicing.

Balsamic Onion Rye Bread

Makes 2 pounds loaf

For the Onions:
- 3 tablespoons olive oil
- 2 tablespoons balsamic vinegar
- 1 large onion (about ¾ pound / 340 g) thinly sliced

For the Dough:
- 1 cup water
- 5 teaspoons sugar
- 3⅓ cups bread flour
- ⅔ cup light or medium rye flour
- 1 tablespoon plus 1 teaspoon gluten
- 2 teaspoons salt
- 2½ teaspoons SAF yeast or 1 tablespoon bread machine yeast

1. To prepare the onions, place the olive oil and the vinegar in a medium sauté pan. Add the onions. Slowly cook over low heat for about 20 minutes, stirring occasionally, until the onions are limp and soggy; do not brown. Pour off any excess liquid into a measuring cup and add water to make the liquid measurement for the dough; you might have 1 to 2 tablespoons, or nothing. Set the onions aside to cool to room temperature. You will have about a full cup of onions.
2. To make the dough, place the dough ingredients in the pan according to the order in the manufacturer's instructions. Set crust on medium or dark and program for the Basic cycle; press Start. When the machine beeps, or between Knead 1 and Knead 2, add the caramelized onions. The dough will initially look dry, so don't be tempted to add liquid; there will be plenty in the onions. If the dough seems too wet 3 minutes after the addition of the onions, add a tablespoon more flour in increments.
3. When the baking cycle ends, immediately remove the bread from the pan and place it on a rack. Let cool to room temperature before slicing.

Chive and Parsley Pull-Apart Rolls

Serves 16

- 1 cup buttermilk
- 6 tablespoons unsalted butter, cut into 6 pieces
- 3⅔ cups all-purpose flour
- 2¼ teaspoons instant yeast
- ⅓ cup granulated sugar
- 1 teaspoon salt
- 3 large egg yolks
- ¼ cup chives, chopped
- ¼ cup parsley, chopped

For the Topping:
- ¼ cup butter, melted

1. Combine the buttermilk and the 6 tablespoons butter in a small saucepan and warm until the butter melts, stirring continuously. Add the packet of instant yeast and allow to stand for five minutes.
2. Mix the egg yolks with a fork and add to the above mixture and blend.
3. Combine the flour, sugar, salt and herbs.
4. Add first the wet then the dry ingredients to your bread machine.
5. Set on Dough cycle and press Start.
6. Lightly grease a 9-by-13-inch glass baking dish.
7. Turn the dough out onto a clean work surface and press down gently. If the dough is too sticky add a little flour to the work surface. Using a bench scraper or a chef's knife, divide the dough into 16 equal pieces
8. Work one piece of dough at a time into a ball; keep the others covered with plastic wrap until ready to bake.
9. Cover the entire baking dish with plastic wrap and let the balls rise in a warm space, about 40 to 60 minutes.
10. Preheat an oven to 375ºF (190ºC) and bake 20 to 25 minutes, or until lightly golden brown.
11. Remove from the oven and brush the tops with melted butter, serve warm.

Prosciutto Bread

Makes 2 pounds loaf

- 1¼ cups water
- ⅓ cup olive oil
- 4 cups bread flour
- 4 ounces (113 g) prosciutto, coarsely chopped
- 1 tablespoon plus 1 teaspoon gluten
- 1 tablespoon plus 1 teaspoon sugar
- 1¼ teaspoons ground black pepper
- ¾ teaspoon salt
- 2 teaspoons SAF yeast or 2½ teaspoons bread machine yeast

1. Place all the ingredients in the pan according to the order in the manufacturer's instructions. Set crust on medium and program for the Basic cycle; press Start.
2. When the baking cycle ends, immediately remove the bread from the pan and place it on a rack. Let cool to room temperature before slicing.

Winter Squash Cloverleaf Rolls

Makes 16 cloverleaf dinner rolls

- 1 (1 1/3-pound / 605-g) winter squash
- ½ cup water
- ½ cup milk
- ⅓ cup butter, melted
- 4½ cups unbleached all-purpose flour
- 3 tablespoons light or dark brown sugar
- Grated zest of 1 orange
- 2 teaspoons salt
- 2¼ teaspoons SAF yeast or 2¾ teaspoons bread machine yeast

1. Preheat the oven to 350ºF (180ºC).
2. If you are using winter squash, wash the squash and cut off the top with a sharp chef's knife. Take care when cutting, because some varieties are very hard. Cut in half and scrape out the seeds and spongy fibers. Leave butternut squash in halves, or cut larger squash into large cubes leaving the skin intact. Place in a baking dish, flesh down, and add a half inch of water. Cover and bake for 1 to 1½ hours, depending on the size of the pieces, or until the flesh is tender when pierced with a knife. Drain, cool, then scoop out the squash flesh and discard the skin. purée the pulp until smooth in a food mill or food processor. You should have about 1 cup. Cool, cover, then refrigerate or freeze until needed. Warm slightly in the microwave before placing in the bread machine.
3. Place all the ingredients in the pan according to the order in the manufacturer's instructions. Program for the Dough cycle; press Start.
4. Grease 16 standard muffin cups (one full pan plus 4 cups in a second pan). When the machine beeps at the end of the cycle, immediately remove the dough and place on a lightly floured work surface; divide into 4 equal portions. Divide each of those pieces into 4 equal portions. Divide each of the 16 portions into 3 portions and form these into small balls about the size of a walnut. You want them all about the same size; this is important or else the rolls will look funny after baking. Arrange 3 balls of dough touching each other in each of the muffin cups. Cover loosely with plastic wrap and let rise until doubled in bulk, about 30 minutes.
5. Meanwhile, preheat the oven to 375ºF (190ºC).
6. Bake for 15 to 18 minutes, or until golden brown. Immediately remove the rolls from the pan. Let cool on racks or serve warm.

Cinnamon Date Walnut Swirl Bread

Serves 16

- 1 cup milk
- 1 large egg
- 4 tablespoons butter
- 4 tablespoons sugar
- 1 teaspoon salt
- 4 cups flour
- $1\frac{2}{3}$ teaspoons yeast

For the Filling:

- ½ cup packed brown sugar
- 1 cup walnuts, chopped
- 1 cup medjool dates, pitted and chopped
- 2 teaspoons cinnamon
- 2 teaspoons clove spice
- $1\frac{1}{3}$ tablespoons butter
- Powdered sugar, sifted

1. Add wet ingredients to the bread maker pan.
2. Mix flour, sugar and salt and add to pan.
3. Make a well in the center of the dry ingredients and add the yeast.
4. Select the Dough cycle and press Start.
5. Punch the dough down and allow it to rest in a warm place.
6. Mix the brown sugar with walnuts, dates and spices; set aside.
7. Roll the dough into a rectangle, on a lightly floured surface.
8. Baste with a tablespoon of butter, add the filling.
9. Start from the short side and roll the dough to form a jelly roll shape.
10. Place the roll into a greased loaf pan and cover.
11. Let it rise in a warm place, until nearly doubled in size; about 30 minutes.
12. Bake at 350ºF (180ºC) for approximately 30 minutes.
13. Cover with foil during the last 10 minutes of cooking.
14. Transfer to a cooling rack for 15 minutes; sprinkle with the powdered sugar and serve.

Chapter 4: Spice and Herb Breads

- 35 Herb Bread
- 35 Cream Cheese Dill Bread
- 36 Garden Herb Bread
- 36 Wildflower Honey Herb Bread
- 37 Buttermilk Lavender Bread
- 37 Cardamom and Turmeric Bread
- 38 Lush Herb Hazelnut Bread
- 38 Cajun Bread
- 39 Black Pepper White Bread
- 39 Spiced Honey Egg Bread
- 40 Easy Herb and Garlic Cream Cheese Bread
- 40 Cinnamon White Bread
- 41 Garlic Bread
- 41 Herbed Parmesan Pesto Bread
- 42 Honey-Lemon Anise Bread
- 42 Cardamom Bread
- 43 Mint Chocolate Bread
- 43 Candied-Ginger Oat Bread
- 44 Lemony Rosemary Hazelnut Bread
- 45 Herb Swirl Semolina Bread
- 46 Pine Nut Basil Bread
- 46 Raisin Breadsticks
- 47 Cinnamon Butter Rolls

Herb Bread

Makes 2 pounds loaf

- 1½ cups fat-free milk
- 3 tablespoons butter, cut into pieces
- 4 cups bread flour
- 1½ tablespoons sugar
- 1 tablespoon plus 1 teaspoon gluten
- 3 tablespoons chopped fresh chives
- 1½ tablespoons dried marjoram
- 1½ teaspoons dried basil
- 1½ teaspoons dried thyme
- 2 teaspoons salt
- 2½ teaspoons SAF yeast or 1 tablespoon bread machine yeast

1. Place all the ingredients in the pan according to the order in the manufacturer's instructions. Set crust on dark and program for the Basic cycle; press Start.
2. When the baking cycle ends, immediately remove the bread from the pan and place it on a rack. Let cool to room temperature before slicing.

Cream Cheese Dill Bread

Makes 2 pounds loaf

- ¾ cup water
- 1 large egg
- 5 ounces (142 g) cream cheese, at room temperature and cut into pieces
- 3 tablespoons unsalted butter, cut into pieces
- 4⅓ cups bread flour
- 1 tablespoon plus 1 teaspoon gluten
- ½ cup finely chopped yellow onion
- 6 tablespoons chopped fresh dill
- 2 teaspoons salt
- 2½ teaspoons SAF yeast or 1 tablespoon bread machine yeast

1. Place all the ingredients in the bread pan according to the order in the manufacturer's instructions. Set crust on medium and program for the Basic cycle; press Start.
2. When the baking cycle ends, immediately remove the bread from the pan and place it on a rack. Let cool to room temperature before slicing.

Garden Herb Bread

Makes 2 pounds loaf

- 1 cup milk
- 1 large egg
- 3 tablespoons unsalted butter, cut into pieces
- 4 cups bread flour
- 1 tablespoon plus 1 teaspoon gluten
- 1 tablespoon plus 1 teaspoon caraway seed, crushed
- 1¼ teaspoons dried sage
- 1¼ teaspoons fresh grated nutmeg
- 2 teaspoons salt
- 2½ teaspoons SAF yeast or 1 tablespoon bread machine yeast

1. Place all the ingredients in the bread pan according to the order in the manufacturer's instructions. Set crust on dark and program for the Basic cycle; press Start.
2. When the baking cycle ends, immediately remove the bread from the pan and place it on a rack. Let cool to room temperature before slicing.

Wildflower Honey Herb Bread

Makes 2 pounds loaf

- 1⅔ cups water
- 2½ tablespoons olive oil
- ¼ cup wildflower honey
- 2¾ cups bread flour
- 1¼ cups whole wheat flour
- ¼ cup light brown sugar
- ¼ cup nonfat dry milk
- 1 tablespoon plus 1 teaspoon gluten
- 2 tablespoons minced fresh parsley
- 2 teaspoons dried basil
- 1¼ teaspoons dried dill weed
- 1¼ teaspoons dried summer savory
- 1 teaspoon dried marjoram
- ¾ teaspoon dried tarragon
- ⅓ teaspoon dried thyme
- 2 teaspoons salt
- 2¼ teaspoons SAF yeast or 2¾ teaspoons bread machine yeast

1. Place all the ingredients in the pan according to the order in the manufacturer's instructions. Set crust on dark and program for the Basic cycle; press Start.
2. When the baking cycle ends, immediately remove the bread from the pan and place it on a rack. Let cool to room temperature before slicing.

Buttermilk Lavender Bread

Makes 2 pounds loaf

- ½ cups water
- 1 cup buttermilk
- ¼ cup olive oil
- 4 cups bread flour
- 3 tablespoons finely chopped fresh lavender leaves
- 1¼ teaspoons finely chopped fresh lavender flowers
- Grated zest of 1 small lemon
- 1 tablespoon plus 1 teaspoon gluten
- 2 teaspoons salt
- 2¼ teaspoons SAF yeast or 2¾ teaspoons bread machine yeast

1. Place all the ingredients in the pan according to the order in the manufacturer's instructions. Set crust on dark and program for the Basic cycle; press Start.
2. When the baking cycle ends, immediately remove the bread from the pan and place it on a rack. Let cool to room temperature before slicing.

Cardamom and Turmeric Bread

Serves 12

- 1 cup lukewarm water
- ⅓ cup lukewarm milk
- 3 tablespoons butter, unsalted
- 3¾ cups unbleached all-purpose flour
- 3 tablespoons sugar
- 1½ teaspoons salt
- 2 tablespoons ground turmeric
- 1 tablespoon ground cardamom
- ½ teaspoon cayenne pepper
- 1½ teaspoons active dry yeast

1. Add liquid ingredients to the bread pan.
2. Measure and add dry ingredients (except yeast) to the bread pan.
3. Make a well in the center of the dry ingredients and add the yeast.
4. Snap the baking pan into the bread maker and close the lid.
5. Choose the Basic cycle, preferred crust color and press Start.
6. When the loaf is done, remove the pan from the machine. After about 5 minutes, gently shake the pan to loosen the loaf and turn it out onto a rack to cool.

Lush Herb Hazelnut Bread

Makes 1½ pounds loaf

- 1¼ cups water
- 1 (14-ounce / 397-g) box white or whole wheat bread machine mix
- ½ cup chopped fresh herbs, any combination of parsley, chervil, basil, marjoram, sage, chives, mint, thyme, or lovage
- ¼ cup chopped hazelnuts
- Grated zest of 1 lemon
- 2 teaspoons gluten
- 1 yeast packet (included in mix)

1. Place all the ingredients in the pan according to the order in the manufacturer's instructions. Set the crust for dark and program for the Basic cycle; press Start.
2. When the baking cycle ends, immediately remove the bread from the pan and place it on a rack. Let cool to room temperature before slicing.

Cajun Bread

Makes 8 slices / 1 pound

- ¾ cup water, at 80ºF (27ºC) to 90ºF (32ºC)
- 1 tablespoon melted butter, cooled
- 2 teaspoons tomato paste
- 1 tablespoon sugar
- 1 teaspoon salt
- 2 tablespoons skim milk powder
- ½ tablespoon Cajun seasoning
- ⅛ teaspoon onion powder
- 2 cups white bread flour
- 1 teaspoon bread machine or instant yeast

1. Place the ingredients in your bread machine as recommended by the manufacturer.
2. Program the machine for Basic/White bread, select light or medium crust, and press Start.
3. When the loaf is done, remove the bucket from the machine.
4. Let the loaf cool for 5 minutes.
5. Gently shake the bucket to remove the loaf, and turn it out onto a rack to cool.

Black Pepper White Bread

Makes 8 slices / 1 pound

- ¾ cup water, at 80ºF (27ºC) to 90ºF (32ºC)
- 1 tablespoon melted butter, cooled
- 1 tablespoon sugar
- ¾ teaspoon salt
- 2 tablespoons skim milk powder
- 1 tablespoon minced chives
- ½ teaspoon garlic powder
- ½ teaspoon cracked black pepper
- 2 cups white bread flour
- ¾ teaspoon bread machine or instant yeast

1. Place the ingredients in your bread machine as recommended by the manufacturer.
2. Program the machine for Basic/White bread, select light or medium crust, and press Start.
3. When the loaf is done, remove the bucket from the machine.
4. Let the loaf cool for 5 minutes.
5. Gently shake the bucket to remove the loaf, and turn it out onto a rack to cool.

Spiced Honey Egg Bread

Makes 8 slices / 1 pound

- ¾ cup milk, at 80ºF (27ºC) to 90ºF (32ºC)
- 1 egg, at room temperature
- 1 tablespoon melted butter, cooled
- 4 teaspoons honey
- ⅔ teaspoon salt
- ⅔ teaspoon ground cinnamon
- ⅓ teaspoon ground cardamom
- ⅓ teaspoon ground nutmeg
- 2 cups white bread flour
- 1⅓ teaspoons bread machine or instant yeast

1. Place the ingredients in your bread machine as recommended by the manufacturer.
2. Program the machine for Basic/White bread, select light or medium crust, and press Start.
3. When the loaf is done, remove the bucket from the machine.
4. Let the loaf cool for 5 minutes.
5. Gently shake the bucket to remove the loaf, and turn it out onto a rack to cool.

Easy Herb and Garlic Cream Cheese Bread

Makes 8 slices / 1 pound

- ⅓ cup water, at 80ºF (27ºC) to 90ºF (32ºC)
- ⅓ cup herb and garlic cream cheese, at room temperature
- 1 egg, at room temperature
- 4 teaspoons melted butter, cooled
- 1 tablespoon sugar
- ⅔ teaspoon salt
- 2 cups white bread flour
- 1 teaspoon bread machine or instant yeast

1. Place the ingredients in your bread machine as recommended by the manufacturer.
2. Program the machine for Basic/White bread, select light or medium crust, and press Start.
3. When the loaf is done, remove the bucket from the machine.
4. Let the loaf cool for 5 minutes.
5. Gently shake the bucket to remove the loaf, and turn it out onto a rack to cool.

Cinnamon White Bread

Makes 8 slices / 1 pound

- ⅔ cup milk, at 80ºF (27ºC) to 90ºF (32ºC)
- 1 egg, at room temperature
- 3 tablespoons melted butter, cooled
- ⅓ cup sugar
- ⅓ teaspoon salt
- 1 teaspoon ground cinnamon
- 2 cups white bread flour
- 1⅓ teaspoons bread machine or active dry yeast

1. Place the ingredients in your bread machine as recommended by the manufacturer.
2. Program the machine for Basic/White bread, select light or medium crust, and press Start.
3. When the loaf is done, remove the bucket from the machine.
4. Let the loaf cool for 5 minutes.
5. Gently shake the bucket to remove the loaf, and turn it out onto a rack to cool.

Garlic Bread

Makes 8 slices / 1 pound

- ⅔ cup milk, at 70ºF (21ºC) to 80ºF (27ºC)
- 1 tablespoon melted butter, cooled
- 2 teaspoons sugar
- 1 teaspoon salt
- 1⅓ teaspoons garlic powder
- 1⅓ teaspoons chopped fresh parsley
- 2 cups white bread flour
- 1⅛ teaspoons bread machine or instant yeast

1. Place the ingredients in your bread machine as recommended by the manufacturer.
2. Program the machine for Basic/White bread, select light or medium crust, and press Start.
3. When the loaf is done, remove the bucket from the machine.
4. Let the loaf cool for 5 minutes.
5. Gently shake the bucket to remove the loaf, and turn it out onto a rack to cool.

Herbed Parmesan Pesto Bread

Makes 8 slices / 1 pound

- ⅔ cup water, at 80ºF (27ºC) to 90ºF (32ºC)
- 1½ tablespoons melted butter, cooled
- 1 teaspoon minced garlic
- ½ tablespoon sugar
- ¾ teaspoon salt
- 2 tablespoons chopped fresh parsley
- ¾ teaspoon chopped fresh basil
- ¼ cup grated Parmesan cheese
- 2 cups white bread flour
- ¾ teaspoon bread machine or active dry yeast

1. Place the ingredients in your bread machine as recommended by the manufacturer.
2. Program the machine for Basic/White bread, select light or medium crust, and press Start.
3. When the loaf is done, remove the bucket from the machine.
4. Let the loaf cool for 5 minutes.
5. Gently shake the bucket to remove the loaf, and turn it out onto a rack to cool.

Honey-Lemon Anise Bread

Makes 8 slices / 1 pound

- ²⁄₃ cup water, at 80ºF (27ºC) to 90ºF (32ºC)
- 1 egg, at room temperature
- 2²⁄₃ tablespoons butter, melted and cooled
- 2²⁄₃ tablespoons honey
- ¹⁄₃ teaspoon salt
- ²⁄₃ teaspoon anise seed
- ²⁄₃ teaspoon lemon zest
- 2 cups white bread flour
- 1¹⁄₃ teaspoons bread machine or instant yeast

1. Place the ingredients in your bread machine as recommended by the manufacturer.
2. Program the machine for Basic/White bread, select light or medium crust, and press Start.
3. When the loaf is done, remove the bucket from the machine.
4. Let the loaf cool for 5 minutes.
5. Gently shake the bucket to remove the loaf, and turn it out onto a rack to cool.

Cardamom Bread

Makes 8 slices / 1 pound

- ½ cup milk, at 80ºF (27ºC) to 90ºF (32ºC)
- 1 egg, at room temperature
- 1 teaspoon melted butter, cooled
- 4 teaspoons honey
- ²⁄₃ teaspoon salt
- ²⁄₃ teaspoon ground cardamom
- 2 cups white bread flour
- ¾ teaspoon bread machine or instant yeast

1. Place the ingredients in your bread machine as recommended by the manufacturer.
2. Program the machine for Basic/White bread, select light or medium crust, and press Start.
3. When the loaf is done, remove the bucket from the machine.
4. Let the loaf cool for 5 minutes.
5. Gently shake the bucket to remove the loaf, and turn it out onto a rack to cool.

Mint Chocolate Bread

Makes 8 slices / 1 pound

- ¾ cup milk, at 80ºF (27ºC) to 90ºF (32ºC)
- ⅛ teaspoon mint extract
- 1 tablespoon butter, melted and cooled
- 2⅔ tablespoons sugar
- ⅔ teaspoon salt
- 1 tablespoon unsweetened cocoa powder
- 2 cups white bread flour
- 1¼ teaspoons bread machine or instant yeast
- ⅓ cup semisweet chocolate chips

1. Place the ingredients in your bread machine as recommended by the manufacturer.
2. Program the machine for Sweet bread, select light or medium crust, and press Start.
3. When the loaf is done, remove the bucket from the machine.
4. Let the loaf cool for 5 minutes.
5. Gently shake the bucket to remove the loaf, and turn it out onto a rack to cool.

Candied-Ginger Oat Bread

Makes 8 slices / 1 pound

- ⅔ cup milk, at 80ºF (27ºC) to 90ºF (32ºC)
- 1 egg, at room temperature
- 2⅔ tablespoons dark molasses
- 4 teaspoons butter, melted and cooled
- ⅓ teaspoon salt
- 2⅔ tablespoons chopped candied ginger
- ⅓ cup quick oats
- 2 cups white bread flour
- 1⅓ teaspoons bread machine or instant yeast

1. Place the ingredients in your bread machine as recommended by the manufacturer.
2. Program the machine for Basic/White bread, select light or medium crust, and press Start.
3. When the loaf is done, remove the bucket from the machine.
4. Let the loaf cool for 5 minutes.
5. Gently shake the bucket to remove the loaf, and turn it out onto a rack to cool.

Lemony Rosemary Hazelnut Bread

Makes 2 pounds loaf

For the Dough:
- 2 cups water
- 3 tablespoons baking soda
- ¾ cup whole hazelnuts
- 1 cup milk
- 1 large egg plus 1 egg yolk
- 3 tablespoons unsalted butter, cut into pieces
- ¼ cup honey
- 3¾ cups bread flour
- 2 teaspoons chopped fresh rosemary
- Grated zest of 1 large lemon
- 1 tablespoon plus 1 teaspoon gluten
- 1¾ teaspoons salt
- 2¼ teaspoons SAF yeast or 2¾ teaspoons bread machine yeast
- 1 cup golden raisins

For the Lemon Icing:
- ¾ cup sifted confectioners' sugar
- 2 tablespoons warm fresh lemon juice

1. Preheat the oven to 350ºF (180ºC).
2. To skin the nuts, bring the 2 cups water to a boil in a saucepan. Add the baking soda and the nuts. Boil for 3 to 5 minutes; the water will turn black. Drain the nuts in a colander and run them under a stream of cold water. Discard the cooking water. Using your fingers, slip off each skin, and place on a clean dish towel. Pat dry and place on a clean baking sheet. Toast the nuts in the oven for 10 to 15 minutes, stirring twice. Cool on the baking sheet. Chop the nuts and set aside.
3. To make the dough, place the remaining dough ingredients, except the hazelnuts and raisins, in the pan according to the order in the manufacturer's instructions. Set crust on medium and program for the Basic cycle; press Start. When the machine beeps, or between Knead 1 and Knead 2, add the raisins and hazelnuts. Add an extra tablespoon or two of water if the dough ball seems dry.
4. When the baking cycle ends, immediately remove the bread from the pan and place it on a rack. Let cool to room temperature before slicing, or drizzle with the lemon icing.
5. To make the lemon icing, if you are using it, whisk the sugar and the lemon juice in a small bowl. Place the rack with the hot bread over a piece of waxed or parchment paper to catch the drips. Drizzle the glaze over the entire loaf, letting some drip down the sides. Let the loaf stand at room temperature until it is completely cool and the glaze is set.

Herb Swirl Semolina Bread

Makes 2 pounds loaf

For the Dough:
- 1 cup water
- 1½ tablespoons olive oil
- ⅔ cup sour cream
- 2¼ cups bread flour
- 1¼ cups semolina flour
- 1 tablespoon sugar
- 1 tablespoon plus 1 teaspoon gluten
- 1¾ teaspoons salt
- 2½ teaspoons SAF yeast or 1 tablespoon bread machine yeast

For the Herb Swirl:
- ⅓ cup chopped fresh flat-leaf parsley
- 3 to 4 tablespoons chopped fresh herbs, such as dill, basil, chervil, marjoram or tarragon
- 1¼ teaspoons dried herb mixture, such as Italian herbs

1. Place all the dough ingredients in the pan according to the order in the manufacturer's instructions.
2. To mix and bake the dough in the machine: Set crust on medium and program for the Basic or Variety cycle; press Start. After Rise 2 of the Basic cycle has ended, press Pause, or when the display shows Shape in the Variety cycle, remove the pan and close the lid. Immediately remove the dough and place it on a lightly floured work surface; pat into a 12-by-8-inch fat rectangle. Brush with 2 tablespoons olive oil. Sprinkle with the parsley and the rest of the herbs, leaving a 1-inch space all the way around. Starting at a short edge, roll up jelly-roll fashion. Tuck the ends under and pinch the bottom seam. Coat the bottom of the dough with cooking spray. Remove the kneading blade and place the dough back in the pan; press Start to continue to rise and bake as programmed.
3. When the baking cycle ends, immediately remove the bread from the pan and place it on a rack. Let cool to room temperature before slicing.
4. To mix the dough in the machine and bake it in the oven: Program the machine for the Dough cycle; press Start. The dough ball will be soft and springy. Follow the shaping instructions in Step 2, then place the loaf in a greased 9-by-5-inch loaf pan instead of putting the loaf back into the bread machine. Spray the top with cooking spray and cover lightly with plastic wrap. Let rise at room temperature until doubled in bulk, about 45 minutes. Bake in a preheated 375ºF (190ºC) oven for 35 to 40 minutes, or until golden brown and the sides have slightly contracted from the pan. Remove the bread from the pan and cool it on a rack.

Pine Nut Basil Bread

Makes 2 pounds loaf

- 1 cup buttermilk
- ½ cup water
- 3 tablespoons butter, cut into pieces
- 3 tablespoons honey
- 4 cups white whole wheat flour
- ⅓ cup chopped fresh basil
- ⅓ cup pine nuts, chopped
- 1 tablespoon plus 1 teaspoon gluten
- 2 teaspoons salt
- 2½ teaspoons SAF yeast or 1 tablespoon bread machine yeast

1. Place all the ingredients in the pan according to the order in the manufacturer's instructions. Set crust on dark and program for the Basic cycle; press Start.
2. When the baking cycle ends, immediately remove the bread from the pan and place it on a rack. Let cool to room temperature before slicing.

Raisin Breadsticks

Serves 16

- 1 cup milk
- 2 tablespoons water
- 1 tablespoon oil
- ¾ teaspoon salt
- 2 tablespoons brown sugar
- 3 cups bread flour
- 1 teaspoon cinnamon
- 1 tablespoon active dry yeast
- ½ cup raisins
- Vanilla icing, for glaze

1. Preheat oven to 475ºF (245ºC).
2. Mix the cinnamon into the bread flour.
3. Add milk, water, oil, salt and brown sugar to the bread maker pan, then add the flour/cinnamon mixture.
4. Make a well in the center of the dry ingredients and add the yeast.
5. Set on Dough cycle and press Start.
6. Take out the dough out and punch down; let rest for 10 minutes.
7. Roll dough into a 12-by-8-inch rectangle.
8. Sprinkle raisins on one half of the dough and gently press them into the dough.
9. Fold the dough in half and gently roll and stretch dough back out into a rectangle.
10. Cut into strips, then twist.
11. Line a baking sheet with parchment paper and bake for 4 minutes.

12. Place on 2 baking sheets that have been lined with parchment paper. Reduce oven temperature to 350ºF (180ºC).
13. Brush breadsticks lightly with water and return to oven and bake 20-25 minutes.
14. Cool on a wire rack.
15. Glaze with vanilla icing and serve.

Cinnamon Butter Rolls

Serves 18

- 1 1/3 cups warm water
- 1 stick of butter, cut into small chunks
- 5 tablespoons sugar
- 1 egg

For the Filling:
- 1 cup sugar
- 1½ tablespoons ground cinnamon

For the Icing:
- 4 cups powdered sugar
- 2 tablespoons melted butter

- 1 teaspoon salt
- 3 cups all-purpose flour
- 1½ cups bread flour
- ¼ cup powdered milk
- 1 tablespoon dry active yeast

- ½ cup butter, softened

- ½ teaspoon vanilla extract
- 4 tablespoons milk

1. Place the ingredients (except yeast) for the dough in your bread machine in the order listed.
2. Make a well in the center of the dry ingredients and add the yeast.
3. Select Dough cycle and press Start.
4. Split kneaded dough into two mounds.
5. On a lightly floured surface, roll one mound of your dough out into a rectangle.
6. Baste with half of the melted butter.
7. Sprinkle half of the cinnamon sugar over the melted butter making sure to cover as much surface with the filling as you can.
8. Starting at one of the short ends of your rectangle of dough, roll it up and brush the outside of roll with melted butter.
9. Slice the dough into about 1-inch pieces.
10. Place pinwheels on greased baking sheet next to one another.
11. Repeat the steps above with the second mound of dough.
12. Cover assembled dough with a light towel and let rise for 25-30 minutes.
13. Bake at 350ºF (180ºC) for 17 minutes or until lightly brown on top.
14. Combine icing ingredients and cover rolls when removed from the oven; allow to cool 10 minutes before serving.

Chapter 5

Sweet Breads

- 50 Nectarine Bread
- 50 Sour Cream Bread
- 51 Barmbrack
- 51 Coffee Dark Bread
- 52 Honey Apple Butter Bread
- 52 Vanilla Peanut Butter Bread
- 53 Granola Bread
- 53 Coffee Cake with Pecans
- 54 Banana-Chocolate Oat Bread
- 55 Sweet Apple Bread
- 55 Almond Milk Bread
- 56 Coconut Pumpkin Bread
- 56 Honey Bread
- 57 Greek Sour Cream Chocolate Bread
- 57 Peanut Butter-Chocolate Banana Bread
- 58 Polish Chocolate Bread
- 59 Monkey Bread with Raisins

Nectarine Bread

Makes 12 to 16 slices / 1½ to 2 pounds

- ½ cup (1 stick) butter, at room temperature
- 2 eggs, at room temperature
- 1 cup sugar
- ¼ cup milk, at room temperature
- 1 teaspoon pure vanilla extract
- 1 cup diced nectarines
- 1¾ cups all-purpose flour
- 1 teaspoon baking soda
- ½ teaspoon salt
- ½ teaspoon ground nutmeg
- ¼ teaspoon baking powder

1. Place the butter, eggs, sugar, milk, vanilla, and nectarines in your bread machine.
2. Program the machine for Quick/Rapid bread and press Start.
3. While the wet ingredients are mixing, stir together the flour, baking soda, salt, nutmeg, and baking powder in a small bowl.
4. After the first fast mixing is done and the machine signals, add the dry ingredients.
5. When the loaf is done, remove the bucket from the machine.
6. Let the loaf cool for 5 minutes.
7. Gently shake the bucket to remove the loaf, and turn it out onto a rack to cool.

Sour Cream Bread

Makes 8 slices / 1 pound

- 6 tablespoons water, at 80ºF (27ºC) to 90ºF (32ºC)
- 6 tablespoons sour cream, at room temperature
- 1½ tablespoons butter, at room temperature
- ¾ tablespoon maple syrup
- ½ teaspoon salt
- 1¾ cups white bread flour
- 1⅛ teaspoons bread machine or instant yeast

1. Place the ingredients in your bread machine as recommended by the manufacturer.
2. Program the machine for Basic/White bread, select light or medium crust, and press Start.
3. When the loaf is done, remove the bucket from the machine.
4. Let the loaf cool for 5 minutes.
5. Gently shake the bucket to remove the loaf, and turn it out onto a rack to cool.

Barmbrack

Makes 8 slices / 1 pound

- ⅔ cup water, at 80ºF (27ºC) to 90ºF (32ºC)
- 1 tablespoon melted butter, cooled
- 2 tablespoons sugar
- 2 tablespoons skim milk powder
- 1 teaspoon salt
- 1 teaspoon dried lemon zest
- ¼ teaspoon ground allspice
- ⅛ teaspoon ground nutmeg
- 2 cups white bread flour
- 1½ teaspoons bread machine or active dry yeast
- ½ cup dried currants

1. Place the ingredients, except the currants, in your bread machine as recommended by the manufacturer.
2. Program the machine for Basic/White bread, select light or medium crust, and press Start.
3. Add the currants when your machine signals or when the second kneading cycle starts.
4. When the loaf is done, remove the bucket from the machine.
5. Let the loaf cool for 5 minutes.
6. Gently shake the bucket to remove the loaf, and turn it out onto a rack to cool.

Coffee Dark Bread

Makes 8 slices / 1 pound

- ½ cup water, at 80ºF (27ºC) to 90ºF (32ºC)
- ¼ cup brewed coffee, at 80ºF (27ºC) to 90ºF (32ºC)
- 1 tablespoon balsamic vinegar
- 1 tablespoon olive oil
- 1 tablespoon dark molasses
- ½ tablespoon light brown sugar
- ½ teaspoon salt
- 1 teaspoon caraway seeds
- 2 tablespoons unsweetened cocoa powder
- ½ cup dark rye flour
- 1¼ cups white bread flour
- 1 teaspoon bread machine or instant yeast

1. Place the ingredients in your bread machine as recommended by the manufacturer.
2. Program the machine for Whole-Wheat/Whole-Grain bread, select light or medium crust, and press Start.
3. When the loaf is done, remove the bucket from the machine.
4. Let the loaf cool for 5 minutes.
5. Gently shake the bucket to remove the loaf, and turn it out onto a rack to cool.

Honey Apple Butter Bread

Makes 8 slices / 1 pound

- ²⁄₃ cup milk, at 80ºF (27ºC) to 90ºF (32ºC)
- ¹⁄₃ cup apple butter, at room temperature
- 4 teaspoons melted butter, cooled
- 2 teaspoons honey
- ²⁄₃ teaspoon salt
- ²⁄₃ cup whole-wheat flour
- 1½ cups white bread flour
- 1 teaspoon bread machine or instant yeast

1. Place the ingredients in your bread machine as recommended by the manufacturer.
2. Program the machine for Basic/White bread, select light or medium crust, and press Start.
3. When the loaf is done, remove the bucket from the machine.
4. Let the loaf cool for 5 minutes.
5. Gently shake the bucket to remove the loaf, and turn it out onto a rack to cool.

Vanilla Peanut Butter Bread

Makes 12 to 16 slices / 1½ to 2 pounds

- 1 cup peanut butter
- 1 cup milk, at 70ºF (21ºC) to 80ºF (27ºC)
- ½ cup packed light brown sugar
- ¼ cup sugar
- ¼ cup (½ stick) butter, at room temperature
- 1 egg, at room temperature
- 2 teaspoons pure vanilla extract
- 2 cups all-purpose flour
- 1 tablespoon baking powder
- ½ teaspoon salt

1. Place the peanut butter, milk, brown sugar, sugar, butter, egg, and vanilla in your bread machine.
2. Program the machine for Quick/Rapid bread and press Start.
3. While the wet ingredients are mixing, stir together the flour, baking powder, and salt in a small bowl.
4. After the first fast mixing is done and the machine signals, add the dry ingredients.
5. When the loaf is done, remove the bucket from the machine.
6. Let the loaf cool for 5 minutes.
7. Gently shake the bucket to remove the loaf, and turn it out onto a rack to cool.

Granola Bread

Makes 8 slices / 1 pound

- ¾ cups milk, at 80ºF (27ºC) to 90ºF (32ºC)
- 2 tablespoons honey
- 1 tablespoon butter, melted and cooled
- ¾ teaspoons salt
- ½ cup whole-wheat flour
- ½ cup prepared granola, crushed
- 1¼ cups white bread flour
- 1 teaspoon bread machine or instant yeast

1. Place the ingredients in your bread machine as recommended by the manufacturer.
2. Program the machine for Basic/White bread, select light or medium crust, and press Start.
3. When the loaf is done, remove the bucket from the machine.
4. Let the loaf cool for 5 minutes.
5. Gently shake the bucket to remove the loaf, and turn it out onto a rack to cool.

Coffee Cake with Pecans

Makes 12 to 16 slices / 1½ to 2 pounds

- ¾ cup buttermilk, at room temperature
- ¾ cup (1½ sticks) butter, at room temperature
- 1 tablespoon instant coffee granules
- 3 eggs, at room temperature
- ¾ cup sugar
- 2 cups all-purpose flour
- ½ tablespoon baking powder
- ½ teaspoon salt
- 1 cup chopped pecans

1. Place the buttermilk, butter, coffee granules, eggs, and sugar in your bread machine.
2. Program the machine for Quick/Rapid bread and press Start.
3. While the wet ingredients are mixing, stir together the flour, baking powder, salt, and pecans in a small bowl.
4. After the first fast mixing is done and the machine signals, add the dry ingredients.
5. When the loaf is done, remove the bucket from the machine.
6. Let the loaf cool for 5 minutes.
7. Gently shake the bucket to remove the loaf, and turn it out onto a rack to cool.

Banana-Chocolate Oat Bread

Makes 12 to 16 slices / 1½ to 2 pounds

- 3 bananas, mashed
- 2 eggs, at room temperature
- ¾ cup packed light brown sugar
- ½ cup (1 stick) butter, at room temperature
- ½ cup sour cream, at room temperature
- ¼ cup sugar
- 1½ teaspoons pure vanilla extract
- 1 cup all-purpose flour
- ½ cup quick oats
- 2 tablespoons unsweetened cocoa powder
- 1 teaspoon baking soda

1. Place the banana, eggs, brown sugar, butter, sour cream, sugar, and vanilla in your bread machine.
2. Program the machine for Quick/Rapid bread and press Start.
3. While the wet ingredients are mixing, stir together the flour, oats, cocoa powder, and baking soda in a small bowl.
4. After the first fast mixing is done and the machine signals, add the dry ingredients.
5. When the loaf is done, remove the bucket from the machine.
6. Let the loaf cool for 5 minutes.
7. Gently shake the bucket to remove the loaf, and turn it out onto a rack to cool.

Sweet Apple Bread

Makes 8 slices / 1 pound

- ¼ cup milk, at 80ºF (27ºC) to 90ºF (32ºC)
- 2 tablespoons apple cider, at room temperature
- 2 tablespoons sugar
- 4 teaspoons melted butter, cooled
- 1 tablespoon honey
- ¼ teaspoon salt
- 2 cups white bread flour
- ¾ teaspoons bread machine or instant yeast
- ⅔ apple, peeled, cored, and finely diced

1. Place the ingredients, except the apple, in your bread machine as recommended by the manufacturer.
2. Program the machine for Basic/White bread, select light or medium crust, and press Start.
3. Add the apple when the machine signals or 5 minutes before the last kneading cycle is complete.
4. When the loaf is done, remove the bucket from the machine.
5. Let the loaf cool for 5 minutes.
6. Gently shake the bucket to remove the loaf, and turn it out onto a rack to cool.

Almond Milk Bread

Makes 8 slices / 1 pound

- ⅓ cup plus 1 tablespoon milk, at 80ºF (27ºC) to 90ºF (32ºC)
- 2 tablespoons melted butter, cooled
- 2 tablespoons sugar
- 1 egg, at room temperature
- 1 teaspoon pure vanilla extract
- ¼ teaspoon pure almond extract
- 1⅔ cups white bread flour
- 1 teaspoon bread machine or instant yeast

1. Place the ingredients in your bread machine as recommended by the manufacturer.
2. Program the machine for Basic/White bread, select light or medium crust, and press Start.
3. When the loaf is done, remove the bucket from the machine.
4. Let the loaf cool for 5 minutes.
5. Gently shake the bucket to remove the loaf, and turn it out onto a rack to cool.

Coconut Pumpkin Bread

Makes 12 to 16 slices / 1½ to 2 pounds

- 1 cup pure canned pumpkin
- ½ cup (1 stick) butter, at room temperature
- 1½ teaspoons pure vanilla extract
- 1 cup sugar
- ½ cup dark brown sugar
- 2 cups all-purpose flour
- ¾ cup sweetened shredded coconut
- 1½ teaspoons ground cinnamon
- 1 teaspoon baking soda
- 1 teaspoon baking powder
- ½ teaspoon ground nutmeg
- ½ teaspoon ground ginger
- ⅛ teaspoon ground allspice

1. Place the pumpkin, butter, vanilla, sugar, and dark brown sugar in your bread machine.
2. Program the machine for Quick/Rapid bread and press Start.
3. After the first fast mixing is done, add the flour, coconut, cinnamon, baking soda, baking powder, nutmeg, ginger, and allspice.
4. When the loaf is done, remove the bucket from the machine.
5. Let the loaf cool for 5 minutes.
6. Gently shake the bucket to remove the loaf, and turn it out onto a rack to cool.

Honey Bread

Makes 8 slices / 1 pound

- ⅔ cup water, at 80°F (27°C) to 90°F (32°C)
- 1 tablespoon honey
- ¾ tablespoon melted butter, cooled
- ½ teaspoon salt
- 1¾ cups white bread flour
- 1 teaspoon bread machine or instant yeast

1. Place the ingredients in your bread machine as recommended by the manufacturer.
2. Program the machine for Basic/White bread, select light or medium crust, and press Start.
3. When the loaf is done, remove the bucket from the machine.
4. Let the loaf cool for 5 minutes.
5. Gently shake the bucket to remove the loaf, and turn it out onto a rack to cool.

Greek Sour Cream Chocolate Bread

Makes 12 to 16 slices / 1½ to 2 pounds

- 1 cup sour cream
- 2 eggs, at room temperature
- 1 cup sugar
- ½ cup (1 stick) butter, at room temperature
- ¼ cup plain Greek yogurt
- 1¾ cups all-purpose flour
- ½ cup unsweetened cocoa powder
- ½ teaspoon baking powder
- ½ teaspoon salt
- 1 cup milk chocolate chips

1. In a small bowl, whisk together the sour cream, eggs, sugar, butter, and yogurt until just combined.
2. Transfer the wet ingredients to the bread machine bucket, and then add the flour, cocoa powder, baking powder, salt, and chocolate chips.
3. Program the machine for Quick/Rapid bread, and press Start.
4. When the loaf is done, stick a knife into it, and if it comes out clean, the loaf is done.
5. If the loaf needs a few more minutes, check the control panel for a Bake Only button and extend the time by 10 minutes.
6. When the loaf is done, remove the bucket from the machine.
7. Let the loaf cool for 5 minutes.
8. Gently shake the bucket to remove the loaf, and turn it out onto a rack to cool.

Peanut Butter-Chocolate Banana Bread

Makes 12 to 16 slices / 1½ to 2 pounds

- 2 bananas, mashed
- 2 eggs, at room temperature
- ½ cup melted butter, cooled
- 2 tablespoons milk, at room temperature
- 1 teaspoon pure vanilla extract
- 2 cups all-purpose flour
- ½ cup sugar
- 1¼ teaspoons baking powder
- ½ teaspoon baking soda
- ½ teaspoon salt
- ½ cup peanut butter chips
- ½ cup semisweet chocolate chips

1. Stir together the bananas, eggs, butter, milk, and vanilla in the bread machine bucket and set it aside.
2. In a medium bowl, toss together the flour, sugar, baking powder, baking soda, salt, peanut butter chips, and chocolate chips.

3. Add the dry ingredients to the bucket.
4. Program the machine for Quick/Rapid bread, and press Start.
5. When the loaf is done, stick a knife into it, and if it comes out clean, the loaf is done.
6. If the loaf needs a few more minutes, check the control panel for a Bake Only button and extend the time by 10 minutes.
7. When the loaf is done, remove the bucket from the machine.
8. Let the loaf cool for 5 minutes.
9. Gently shake the bucket to remove the loaf, and turn it out onto a rack to cool.

Polish Chocolate Bread

Makes 8 slices / 1 pound

- ⅔ cup milk, at 80ºF (27ºC) to 90ºF (32ºC)
- 1 egg, at room temperature
- 1½ tablespoons melted butter, cooled
- 1 teaspoon pure vanilla extract
- 2 tablespoons light brown sugar
- 1 tablespoon unsweetened cocoa powder
- ½ teaspoon salt
- 2 cups white bread flour
- 1 teaspoon bread machine or instant yeast
- ¼ cup semisweet chocolate chips
- ¼ cup white chocolate chips

1. Place the ingredients, except the chocolate chips, in your bread machine as recommended by the manufacturer.
2. Program the machine for Basic/White bread, select light or medium crust, and press Start.
3. When the machine signals, add the chocolate chips, or put them in the nut/raisin hopper and the machine will add them automatically.
4. When the loaf is done, remove the bucket from the machine.
5. Let the loaf cool for 5 minutes.
6. Gently shake the bucket to remove the loaf, and turn it out onto a rack to cool.

Monkey Bread with Raisins

Serves 12 to 15

- 1 cup water
- 1 cup butter, unsalted
- 2 tablespoons butter, softened
- 3 cups all-purpose flour
- 1 teaspoon ground cinnamon
- 1 teaspoon salt
- ¼ cup white sugar
- 2½ teaspoons active dry yeast
- 1 cup brown sugar, packed
- 1 cup raisins
- Flour, for surface

1. Add ingredients, except 1 cup butter, brown sugar, raisins and yeast, to bread maker pan in order listed above.
2. Make a well in the center of the dry ingredients and add the yeast. Make sure that no liquid comes in contact with the yeast.
3. Select Dough cycle and press Start.
4. Place finished dough on floured surface and knead 10 times.
5. Melt one cup of butter in small saucepan.
6. Stir in brown sugar and raisins and mix until smooth. Remove from heat.
7. Cut dough into one inch chunks.
8. Drop one chunk at a time into the butter sugar mixture. Thoroughly coat dough pieces, then layer them loosely in a greased Bundt pan.
9. Let rise in a warm, draft-free space; about 15 to 20 minutes.
10. Bake at 375ºF (190ºC) for 20 to 25 minutes or until golden brown.
11. Remove from oven, plate, and serve warm.

Chapter 6 — Sourdough Breads

- 62 Pecan-Cranberry Sourdough Bread
- 62 No-Yeast Whole-Wheat Sourdough Starter
- 63 Sourdough Bread
- 63 Baisc Whole-Wheat Sourdough Bread
- 64 Multigrain Cereal Sourdough Bread
- 64 Faux Apple Cider Sourdough Bread
- 65 Milk Sourdough Bread
- 65 Citrus Sourdough Egg Bread
- 66 Skim Milk Sourdough Bread
- 66 Beer Sourdough Bread
- 67 Honey Sourdough Bread
- 67 Cheddar Cheese Sourdough Oat Bread
- 68 Herbed Sourdough Bread
- 68 Sourdough Starter
- 69 No-Yeast Sourdough Starter
- 69 Chocolate Sourdough Bread wtih Pistachios

Pecan-Cranberry Sourdough Bread

Makes 8 slices / 1 pound

- 1 1/3 cups No-Yeast Sourdough Starter, fed, active, and at room temperature
- 4 teaspoons water, at 80°F (27°C) to 90°F (32°C)
- 4 teaspoons melted butter, cooled
- 1 1/3 teaspoons sugar
- 1 teaspoon salt
- 1/4 teaspoon ground cinnamon
- 1 2/3 cups white bread flour
- 1 teaspoon bread machine or instant yeast
- 1/4 cup dried cranberries
- 1/4 cup chopped pecans

1. Place the ingredients, except the cranberries and pecans, in your bread machine as recommended by the manufacturer.
2. Program the machine for Basic/White bread, select light or medium crust, and press Start.
3. Add the cranberries and pecans when the machine signals or 5 minutes before the second kneading cycle is finished.
4. When the loaf is done, remove the bucket from the machine.
5. Let the loaf cool for 5 minutes.
6. Gently shake the bucket to remove the loaf, and turn it out onto a rack to cool.

No-Yeast Whole-Wheat Sourdough Starter

Makes 2 cups (32 servings)

- 1 cup whole-wheat flour, divided
- 1 cup chlorine-free bottled water, at room temperature, divided
- 1/2 teaspoon honey

1. Stir together 1/2 cup of flour, 1/2 cup of water, and the honey in a large glass bowl with a wooden spoon.
2. Loosely cover the bowl with plastic wrap and place it in a warm area for 5 days, stirring at least twice a day.
3. After 5 days, stir in the remaining 1/2 cup of flour and 1/2 cup of water.
4. Cover the bowl loosely again with plastic wrap and place it in a warm area.
5. When the starter has bubbles and foam on top, it is ready to use.
6. Store the starter in the refrigerator in a covered glass jar, and stir it before using.
7. If you use half, replenish the starter with 1/2 cup flour and 1/2 cup water.

Sourdough Bread

Makes 8 slices / 1 pound

- 1 1/3 cups Sourdough Starter, fed, active, and at room temperature
- 4 teaspoons water, at 80ºF (27ºC) to 90ºF (32ºC)
- 4 teaspoons melted butter, cooled
- 1 1/3 teaspoons sugar
- 1 teaspoon salt
- 1 2/3 cups white bread flour
- 1 teaspoon bread machine or instant yeast

1. Place the ingredients in your bread machine as recommended by the manufacturer.
2. Program the machine for Basic/White bread, select light or medium crust, and press Start.
3. When the loaf is done, remove the bucket from the machine.
4. Let the loaf cool for 5 minutes.
5. Gently shake the bucket to remove the loaf, and turn it out onto a rack to cool.

Baisc Whole-Wheat Sourdough Bread

Makes 8 slices / 1 pound

- 2/3 cups water, at 80ºF (27ºC) to 90ºF (32ºC)
- 2/3 cup No-Yeast Whole-Wheat Sourdough Starter, fed, active, and at room temperature
- 4 teaspoons melted butter, cooled
- 2 teaspoons sugar
- 1 teaspoon salt
- 2 cups whole-wheat flour
- 1 1/4 teaspoons bread machine or instant yeast

1. Place the ingredients in your bread machine as recommended by the manufacturer.
2. Program the machine for Whole-Wheat/Whole-Grain bread, select light or medium crust, and press Start.
3. When the loaf is done, remove the bucket from the machine.
4. Let the loaf cool for 5 minutes.
5. Gently shake the bucket to remove the loaf, and turn it out onto a rack to cool.

Multigrain Cereal Sourdough Bread

Makes 8 slices / 1 pound

- 1/3 cup plus 1 tablespoon water, at 80ºF (27ºC) to 90ºF (32ºC)
- 1/2 cup Sourdough Starter, fed, active, and at room temperature
- 4 teaspoons melted butter, cooled
- 1 2/3 tablespoons sugar
- 1/2 teaspoon salt
- 1/2 cup multigrain cereal
- 1 3/4 cups white bread flour
- 1 teaspoon bread machine or instant yeast

1. Place the ingredients in your bread machine as recommended by the manufacturer.
2. Program the machine for Whole-Wheat/Whole-Grain bread, select light or medium crust, and press Start.
3. When the loaf is done, remove the bucket from the machine.
4. Let the loaf cool for 5 minutes.
5. Gently shake the bucket to remove the loaf, and turn it out onto a rack to cool.

Faux Apple Cider Sourdough Bread

Makes 8 slices / 1 pound

- 1/2 cup plus 1 tablespoon water, at 80ºF (27ºC) to 90ºF (32ºC)
- 1/4 cup sour cream, at room temperature
- 1 1/2 tablespoons melted butter, cooled
- 1 tablespoon apple cider vinegar
- 1/2 tablespoon sugar
- 1/2 teaspoon salt
- 2 cups white bread flour
- 3/4 teaspoon bread machine or instant yeast

1. Place the ingredients in your bread machine as recommended by the manufacturer.
2. Program the machine for French bread, select light or medium crust, and press Start.
3. When the loaf is done, remove the bucket from the machine.
4. Let the loaf cool for 5 minutes.
5. Gently shake the bucket to remove the loaf, and turn it out onto a rack to cool.

Milk Sourdough Bread

Makes 8 slices / 1 pound

- 1 cup Sourdough Starter or No-Yeast Sourdough Starter, fed, active, and at room temperature
- ¼ cup milk, at 80ºF (27ºC) to 90ºF (32ºC)
- 2 tablespoons olive oil
- 1 tablespoon honey
- ⅔ teaspoon salt
- 2 cups white bread flour
- ¾ teaspoon bread machine or instant yeast

1. Place the ingredients in your bread machine as recommended by the manufacturer.
2. Program the machine for Basic/White bread, select light or medium crust, and press Start.
3. When the loaf is done, remove the bucket from the machine.
4. Let the loaf cool for 5 minutes.
5. Gently shake the bucket to remove the loaf, and turn it out onto a rack to cool.

Citrus Sourdough Egg Bread

Makes 8 slices / 1 pound

- ½ cup Sourdough Starter or No-Yeast Sourdough Starter, fed, active, and at room temperature
- ½ cup water, at 80ºF (27ºC) to 90ºF (32ºC)
- 1 small egg, at room temperature
- 2 tablespoons butter, melted and cooled
- ¼ cup honey
- 1 teaspoon salt
- 1⅓ teaspoons lemon zest
- 1 teaspoon lime zest
- ¼ cup wheat germ
- 2 cups white bread flour
- 1⅛ teaspoons bread machine or instant yeast

1. Place the ingredients in your bread machine as recommended by the manufacturer.
2. Program the machine for Basic/White bread, select light or medium crust, and press Start.
3. When the loaf is done, remove the bucket from the machine.
4. Let the loaf cool for 5 minutes.
5. Gently shake the bucket to remove the loaf, and turn it out onto a rack to cool.

Skim Milk Sourdough Bread

Makes 8 slices / 1 pound

- ¾ cup Sourdough Starter or No-Yeast Sourdough Starter, fed, active, and at room temperature
- ⅓ cup water, at 80°F (27°C) to 90°F (32°C)
- 1½ tablespoons olive oil
- 1 teaspoon salt
- 4 teaspoons sugar
- 1 tablespoon skim milk powder
- ¼ cup whole-wheat flour
- 1¾ cups white bread flour
- 1⅛ teaspoons bread machine or instant yeast

1. Place the ingredients in your bread machine as recommended by the manufacturer.
2. Program the machine for French bread, select light or medium crust, and press Start.
3. When the loaf is done, remove the bucket from the machine.
4. Let the loaf cool for 5 minutes.
5. Gently shake the bucket to remove the loaf, and turn it out onto a rack to cool.

Beer Sourdough Bread

Makes 8 slices / 1 pound

- ⅔ cup Sourdough Starter or No-Yeast Sourdough Starter, fed, active, and at room temperature
- ⅓ cup dark beer, at 80°F (27°C) to 90°F (32°C)
- 1 tablespoon melted butter, cooled
- 1½ teaspoons sugar
- ¾ teaspoon salt
- 1¾ cups white bread flour
- ¾ teaspoon bread machine or instant yeast

1. Place the ingredients in your bread machine as recommended by the manufacturer.
2. Program the machine for French bread, select light or medium crust, and press Start.
3. When the loaf is done, remove the bucket from the machine.
4. Let the loaf cool for 5 minutes.
5. Gently shake the bucket to remove the loaf, and turn it out onto a rack to cool.

Honey Sourdough Bread

Makes 8 slices / 1 pound

- ⅔ cup Sourdough Starter, fed, active, and at room temperature
- ⅓ cup water, at 80ºF (27ºC) to 90ºF (32ºC)
- 4 teaspoons honey
- 1 teaspoon salt
- 2 cups white bread flour
- ¾ teaspoon bread machine or instant yeast

1. Place the ingredients in your bread machine as recommended by the manufacturer.
2. Program the machine for Basic/White bread, select light or medium crust, and press Start.
3. When the loaf is done, remove the bucket from the machine.
4. Let the loaf cool for 5 minutes.
5. Gently shake the bucket to remove the loaf, and turn it out onto a rack to cool.

Cheddar Cheese Sourdough Oat Bread

Makes 8 slices / 1 pound

- 1 tablespoon melted butter, cooled
- ⅔ cup Sourdough Starter or No-Yeast Sourdough Starter, fed, active, and at room temperature
- ¼ cup water, at 80ºF (27ºC) to 90ºF (32ºC)
- 2⅔ teaspoons sugar
- ⅔ teaspoon salt
- ⅓ cup grated aged Cheddar cheese
- ⅔ cup whole-wheat flour
- 2⅔ tablespoons oat bran
- ¾ cup plus 1 tablespoon white bread flour
- 1 teaspoon bread machine or instant yeast

1. Place the ingredients in your bread machine as recommended by the manufacturer.
2. Program the machine for Basic/White bread, select light or medium crust, and press Start.
3. When the loaf is done, remove the bucket from the machine.
4. Let the loaf cool for 5 minutes.
5. Gently shake the bucket to remove the loaf, and turn it out onto a rack to cool.

Herbed Sourdough Bread

Makes 8 slices / 1 pound

- 1 1/3 cups No-Yeast Sourdough Starter, fed, active, and at room temperature
- 4 teaspoons water, at 80ºF (27ºC) to 90ºF (32ºC)
- 4 teaspoons melted butter, cooled
- 1 1/3 teaspoons sugar
- 1 teaspoon salt
- 1 teaspoon chopped fresh basil
- 1 teaspoon chopped fresh oregano
- ½ teaspoon chopped fresh thyme
- 1 2/3 cups white bread flour
- 1 teaspoon bread machine or instant yeast

1. Place the ingredients in your bread machine as recommended by the manufacturer.
2. Program the machine for Basic/White bread, select light or medium crust, and press Start.
3. When the loaf is done, remove the bucket from the machine.
4. Let the loaf cool for 5 minutes.
5. Gently shake the bucket to remove the loaf, and turn it out onto a rack to cool.

Sourdough Starter

Makes 2 cups (32 servings)

- 2½ teaspoons active dry yeast
- 2 cups water, at 100ºF (38ºC) to 110ºF (43ºC)
- 2 cups all-purpose flour

1. In a large nonmetallic bowl, stir together the yeast, water, and flour.
2. Cover the bowl loosely and place it in a warm place to ferment for 4 to 8 days, stirring several times per day.
3. When the starter is bubbly and has a pleasant sour smell, it is ready to use.
4. Store the starter covered in the refrigerator until you wish to use it.

No-Yeast Sourdough Starter

Makes 4 cups (64 servings)

- 2 cups all-purpose flour
- 2 cups chlorine-free bottled water, at room temperature

1. Stir together the flour and water in a large glass bowl with a wooden spoon.
2. Loosely cover the bowl with plastic wrap and place it in a warm area for 3 to 4 days, stirring at least twice a day, or until bubbly.
3. Store the starter in the refrigerator in a covered glass jar, and stir it before using.
4. Replenish your starter by adding back the same amount you removed, in equal parts flour and water.

Chocolate Sourdough Bread wtih Pistachios

Makes 8 slices / 1 pound

- 1 1/3 cups No-Yeast Sourdough Starter, fed, active, and at room temperature
- 4 teaspoons water, at 80°F (27°C) to 90°F (32°C)
- 4 teaspoons melted butter, cooled
- 1/2 teaspoon pure vanilla extract
- 1 1/3 teaspoons sugar
- 1 teaspoon salt
- 1/4 teaspoon ground cinnamon
- 2 tablespoons unsweetened cocoa powder
- 1 2/3 cups white bread flour
- 1 teaspoon bread machine or instant yeast
- 1/4 cup semisweet chocolate chips
- 1/4 cup chopped pistachios
- 1/4 cup raisins

1. Place the ingredients, except the chocolate chips, pistachios, and raisins, in your bread machine as recommended by the manufacturer.
2. Program the machine for Basic/White bread, select light or medium crust, and press Start.
3. Add the chocolate chips, pistachios, and raisins when the machine signals or 5 minutes before the second kneading cycle is finished.
4. When the loaf is done, remove the bucket from the machine.
5. Let the loaf cool for 5 minutes.
6. Gently shake the bucket to remove the loaf, and turn it out onto a rack to cool.

Chapter 7

Nut and Seed Breads

72	Buttermilk Nutmeat Bread
72	Oat and Sunflower Seed Bread
73	Walnut Bread
73	Sunflower and Sesame Seed Bread
74	Pecan Bread
74	Honey Flaxseed Bread
75	Triple Seed Bread
75	Nut and Seed Bread
76	Coconut Bread
76	Hazelnut Bread
77	Sesame and Chia Seed Bread
77	Rye Seed Bread
78	Lush Seed and Oat Bread
78	Almond-Coconut Pumpkin Bread
79	Sesame and FlaxSeed Bread with Raisins

Buttermilk Nutmeat Bread

Makes 2 pounds loaf

- 1 cup nutmeat pieces
- 1 2/3 cups buttermilk
- ½ cup nut oil
- 4 cups bread flour
- 1½ tablespoons dark brown sugar
- 1 tablespoon plus 1 teaspoon gluten
- 2 teaspoons salt
- 1 tablespoon SAF yeast or 1 tablespoon plus ½ teaspoon bread machine yeast

1. Preheat the oven to 350ºF (180ºC).
2. Spread the nuts evenly on a baking sheet. Bake until lightly toasted, about 5 to 7 minutes. Remove from the oven and let cool.
3. Place the ingredients, except the nuts, in the pan according to the order in the manufacturer's instructions. Set crust on medium or dark and program for the Basic cycle; press Start. When the machine beeps or between Knead 1 and Knead 2, add the nuts. Test the dough with your fingers. If it is very firm and dry, maybe even lumpy, add another tablespoon of buttermilk to soften it up a bit.
4. When the baking cycle ends, immediately remove the bread from the pan and place it on a rack. Let cool to room temperature before slicing.

Oat and Sunflower Seed Bread

Makes 2 pounds loaf

- 2/3 cup water
- 1 cup buttermilk
- 1 large egg
- 2 tablespoons butter, cut into pieces
- 3 tablespoons honey
- 1½ tablespoons molasses
- 3 1/3 cups bread flour
- 2/3 cup rolled oats
- 2/3 cup whole wheat flour
- 2/3 cup raw sunflower seeds
- 1 tablespoon plus 1 teaspoon gluten
- 2 teaspoons salt
- 2¼ teaspoons SAF yeast or 2¾ teaspoons bread machine yeast

1. Place all the ingredients in the bread pan according to the order in the manufacturer's instructions. Set crust on medium and program for the Basic cycle; press Start.
2. When the baking cycle ends, immediately remove the bread from the pan and place it on a rack. Let cool to room temperature before slicing.

Walnut Bread

Makes 2 pounds loaf

- 1 cup walnut pieces
- 1 1/3 cups water
- 2 large egg whites, lightly beaten
- 2 tablespoons butter, cut into pieces
- 4 cups bread flour
- 3 tablespoons sugar
- 3 tablespoons nonfat dry milk
- 1 tablespoon plus 1 teaspoon gluten
- 1 teaspoon salt
- 2 teaspoons SAF yeast or 2½ teaspoons bread machine yeast

1. Preheat the oven to 350ºF (180ºC).
2. Spread the walnuts on a baking sheet and place in the center of the oven for 4 minutes to toast lightly. Set aside to cool.
3. Place the ingredients, except the walnuts, in the pan according to the order in the manufacturer's instructions. Set crust on medium and program for the Basic cycle; press Start. When the machine beeps, or between Knead 1 and Knead 2, add the walnuts.
4. When the baking cycle ends, immediately remove the bread from the pan and place it on a rack. Let cool to room temperature before slicing.

Sunflower and Sesame Seed Bread

Makes 8 slices / 1 pound

- ¾ cup water, at 80ºF (27ºC) to 90ºF (32ºC)
- 1 tablespoon honey
- 1 tablespoon melted butter, cooled
- ½ teaspoon salt
- 2 cups whole-wheat flour
- ½ cup white bread flour
- 2 tablespoons raw sunflower seeds
- 1 tablespoon sesame seeds
- 1 teaspoon bread machine or instant yeast

1. Place the ingredients in your bread machine as recommended by the manufacturer.
2. Program the machine for Whole-Wheat/Whole-Grain bread, select light or medium crust, and press Start.
3. When the loaf is done, remove the bucket from the machine.
4. Let the loaf cool for 5 minutes.
5. Gently shake the bucket to remove the loaf, and turn it out onto a rack to cool.

Pecan Bread

Makes 8 slices / 1 pound

- ²⁄₃ cup milk, at 70ºF (21ºC) to 80ºF (27ºC)
- 4 teaspoons melted butter, cooled
- 1 egg, at room temperature
- 4 teaspoons sugar
- ²⁄₃ teaspoon salt
- 2 cups white bread flour
- 1 teaspoon bread machine or instant yeast
- ²⁄₃ cup chopped pecans, toasted

1. Place the ingredients, except the pecans, in your bread machine as recommended by the manufacturer.
2. Program the machine for Basic/White bread, select light or medium crust, and press Start.
3. When the machine signals, add the pecans, or put them in a nut/raisin hopper and the machine will add them automatically.
4. When the loaf is done, remove the bucket from the machine.
5. Let the loaf cool for 5 minutes.
6. Gently shake the bucket to remove the loaf, and turn it out onto a rack to cool.

Honey Flaxseed Bread

Makes 8 slices / 1 pound

- ¾ cup milk, at 80ºF (27ºC) to 90ºF (32ºC)
- 1 tablespoon melted butter, cooled
- 1 tablespoon honey
- ¾ teaspoon salt
- 2 tablespoons flaxseed
- 2 cups white bread flour
- ¾ teaspoon bread machine or instant yeast

1. Place the ingredients in your bread machine as recommended by the manufacturer.
2. Program the machine for Basic/White bread, select light or medium crust, and press Start.
3. When the loaf is done, remove the bucket from the machine.
4. Let the loaf cool for 5 minutes.
5. Gently shake the bucket to remove the loaf, and turn it out onto a rack to cool.

Triple Seed Bread

Makes 8 slices / 1 pound

- ¾ cup milk, at 80ºF (27ºC) to 90ºF (32ºC)
- 1 tablespoon melted butter, cooled
- 1 tablespoon honey
- ½ teaspoon salt
- 2 tablespoons flaxseed
- 2 tablespoons sesame seeds
- 1 tablespoon poppy seeds
- ¾ cup whole-wheat flour
- 1¼ cups white bread flour
- 1¼ teaspoons bread machine or instant yeast

1. Place the ingredients in your bread machine as recommended by the manufacturer.
2. Program the machine for Basic/White bread, select light or medium crust, and press Start.
3. When the loaf is done, remove the bucket from the machine.
4. Let the loaf cool for 5 minutes.
5. Gently shake the bucket to remove the loaf, and turn it out onto a rack to cool.

Nut and Seed Bread

Makes 8 slices / 1 pound

- 1 cup water, at 80ºF (27ºC) to 90ºF (32ºC)
- 4 teaspoons melted butter, cooled
- 2 teaspoons sugar
- 1 teaspoon salt
- ¾ cup plus 1 tablespoon whole-wheat flour
- 1⅓ cups white bread flour
- 1 teaspoon bread machine or instant yeast
- 4 teaspoons chopped almonds
- 4 teaspoons chopped pecans
- 4 teaspoons sunflower seeds

1. Place the ingredients, except the almonds, pecans, and seeds, in your bread machine as recommended by the manufacturer.
2. Program the machine for Basic/White bread, select light or medium crust, and press Start.
3. When the machine signals, add the nuts and seeds, or put them in the nut/raisin hopper and let the machine add them automatically.
4. When the loaf is done, remove the bucket from the machine.
5. Let the loaf cool for 5 minutes.
6. Gently shake the bucket to remove the loaf, and turn it out onto a rack to cool.

Coconut Bread

Makes 8 slices / 1 pound

- ²⁄₃ cup milk, at 80ºF (27ºC) to 90ºF (32ºC)
- 1 egg, at room temperature
- 1 tablespoon melted butter, cooled
- 1¹⁄₃ teaspoons pure coconut extract
- 1²⁄₃ tablespoons sugar
- ½ teaspoon salt
- ¹⁄₃ cup sweetened shredded coconut
- 2 cups white bread flour
- 1 teaspoon bread machine or instant yeast

1. Place the ingredients in your bread machine as recommended by the manufacturer.
2. Program the machine for Sweet bread, select light or medium crust, and press Start.
3. When the loaf is done, remove the bucket from the machine.
4. Let the loaf cool for 5 minutes.
5. Gently shake the bucket to remove the loaf, and turn it out onto a rack to cool.

Hazelnut Bread

Makes 8 slices / 1 pound

- ²⁄₃ cup milk, at 70ºF (21ºC) to 80ºF (27ºC)
- 1 egg, at room temperature
- 2½ tablespoons melted butter, cooled
- 2 tablespoons honey
- ½ teaspoon pure vanilla extract
- ½ teaspoon salt
- ½ cup finely ground toasted hazelnuts
- 2 cups white bread flour
- 1 teaspoon bread machine or instant yeast

1. Place the ingredients in your bread machine as recommended by the manufacturer.
2. Program the machine for Basic/White bread, select light or medium crust, and press Start.
3. When the loaf is done, remove the bucket from the machine.
4. Let the loaf cool for 5 minutes.
5. Gently shake the bucket to remove the loaf, and turn it out onto a rack to cool.

Sesame and Chia Seed Bread

Makes 8 slices / 1 pound

- ¾ cup water, at 80ºF (27ºC) to 90ºF (32ºC)
- 1 tablespoon melted butter, cooled
- 1 tablespoon sugar
- ¾ teaspoon salt
- ⅓ cup ground chia seeds
- 1 tablespoon sesame seeds
- 1⅔ cups white bread flour
- 1 teaspoon bread machine or instant yeast

1. Place the ingredients in your bread machine as recommended by the manufacturer.
2. Program the machine for Basic/White bread, select light or medium crust, and press Start.
3. When the loaf is done, remove the bucket from the machine.
4. Let the loaf cool for 5 minutes.
5. Gently shake the bucket to remove the loaf, and turn it out onto a rack to cool.

Rye Seed Bread

Makes 2 pounds loaf

- ¾ teaspoon dill seed
- ¾ teaspoon poppy seeds
- ⅓ teaspoon celery seeds
- 1⅛ cups plus 1 tablespoon water
- 1 large egg
- 2 tablespoons minced shallot
- 1½ tablespoons molasses
- 3 cups bread flour
- 1 cup medium or dark rye flour
- 1 tablespoon plus 1 teaspoon gluten
- 1⅓ teaspoons caraway seed
- 2¼ teaspoons salt
- 2½ teaspoons SAF yeast or 1 tablespoon bread machine yeast

1. Using a mortar and pestle, combine the dill seeds, poppy seeds, and celery seeds and crush them together coarsely. Or place the seeds between 2 sheets of waxed paper and crush them with a rolling pin.
2. Place all the ingredients in the pan according to the order in the manufacturer's instructions, adding the crushed seeds with the dry ingredients. Set crust on dark and program for the Basic cycle; press Start.
3. When the baking cycle ends, immediately remove the bread from the pan and place it on a rack. Let cool to room temperature before slicing.

Lush Seed and Oat Bread

Makes 8 slices / 1 pound

- ¾ cup water, at 80ºF (27ºC) to 90ºF (32ºC)
- 2 tablespoons melted butter, cooled
- 2 tablespoons light brown sugar
- 1 teaspoon salt
- 2 tablespoons raw sunflower seeds
- 2 tablespoons pumpkin seeds
- 1 tablespoon sesame seeds
- ½ teaspoon anise seeds
- ¾ cup quick oats
- 1½ cups white bread flour
- 1 teaspoon bread machine or instant yeast

1. Place the ingredients in your bread machine as recommended by the manufacturer.
2. Program the machine for Basic/White bread, select light or medium crust, and press Start.
3. When the loaf is done, remove the bucket from the machine.
4. Let the loaf cool for 5 minutes.
5. Gently shake the bucket to remove the loaf, and turn it out onto a rack to cool.

Almond-Coconut Pumpkin Bread

Serves 12

- ⅓ cup vegetable oil
- 3 large eggs
- 1½ cups canned pumpkin purée
- 1 cup sugar
- 1½ teaspoons baking powder
- ½ teaspoon baking soda
- ¼ teaspoon salt
- 1 tablespoon allspice
- 3 cups all-purpose flour
- ½ cup coconut flakes, plus a small handful for the topping
- ⅔ cup slivered almonds, plus a tablespoonful for the topping
- Non-stick cooking spray

1. Spray bread maker pan with non-stick cooking spray.
2. Mix oil, eggs, and pumpkin in a large mixing bowl.
3. Mix remaining ingredients together in a separate mixing bowl.
4. Add wet ingredients to bread maker pan, and dry ingredients on top.
5. Select Dough cycle and press Start.
6. Open lid and sprinkle top of bread with reserved coconut and almonds.
7. Set to Rapid for 1 hour 30 minutes and bake.
8. Cool for 10 minutes on a wire rack before serving.

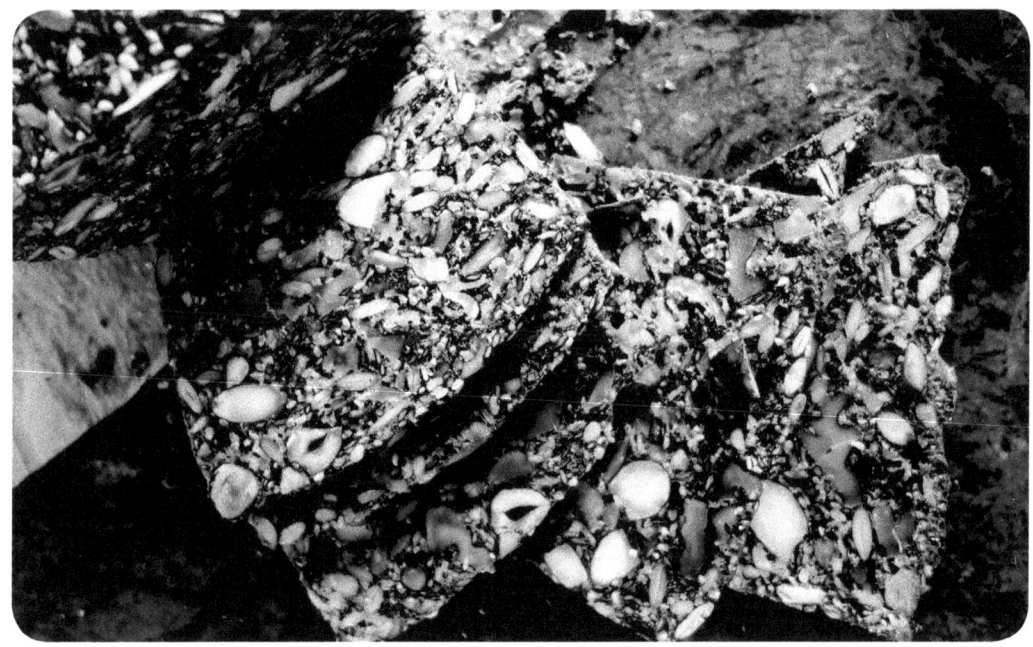

Sesame and FlaxSeed Bread with Raisins

Makes 8 slices / 1 pound

- ¾ cup milk, at 80ºF (27ºC) to 90ºF (32ºC)
- 1 tablespoon melted butter, cooled
- 1 tablespoon honey
- ½ teaspoon salt
- 2 tablespoons flaxseed
- 2 tablespoons sesame seeds
- ¾ cup whole-wheat flour
- 1¼ cups white bread flour
- 1¼ teaspoons bread machine or instant yeast
- ¼ cup raisins

1. Place the ingredients, except the raisins, in your bread machine as recommended by the manufacturer.
2. Program the machine for Basic/White bread, select light or medium crust, and press Start.
3. Add the raisins when your bread machine signals, or place the raisins in the raisin/nut hopper and let the machine add them.
4. When the loaf is done, remove the bucket from the machine.
5. Let the loaf cool for 5 minutes.
6. Gently shake the bucket to remove the loaf, and turn it out onto a rack to cool.

Specialty Breads

- 82 Classic Italian Cornmeal Bread
- 82 Pan de Muertos
- 83 Sweet Mexican Bread
- 83 Authentic Challah
- 84 Russian Caraway and Fennel Rye Bread
- 84 Russian Coriander and Caraway Rye Bread
- 85 Hawaiian Pineapple Bread
- 85 Easter Bread
- 86 British Cinnamon Raisin Hot Cross Buns
- 86 Za'atar Bread
- 87 Portuguese Cornmeal Bread
- 87 Panettone
- 88 Simple Amish Bread
- 88 Fiji Sweet Potato Bread

Classic Italian Cornmeal Bread

Serves: 16

- 4 cups unbleached flour
- 1 tablespoon light brown sugar
- 1 1/3 cups warm water
- 1½ teaspoons salt
- 1½ teaspoons olive oil
- 1 package active dry yeast
- 1 egg
- 1 tablespoon water
- 2 tablespoons cornmeal

1. Add flour, brown sugar, warm water, salt, olive oil and yeast to the bread maker pan.
2. Select Dough cycle and press Start.
3. Punch down the dough and turn it out onto a lightly floured surface.
4. Form into two loaves and place them seam-side down on a cutting board.
5. Generously sprinkle with cornmeal and cover the loaves with a damp cloth.
6. Let rise until doubled in volume, about 40 minutes.
7. Beat egg and 1 tablespoon of water in a small mixing bowl.
8. Baste loaves with egg wash.
9. Cut down the center of loaves with a sharp knife.
10. Bake in 475ºF (245ºC) preheated oven for 30 to 35 minutes, or until loaves sound hollow when tapped on the bottom.
11. Transfer to cooling rack for 15 minutes before serving.

Pan de Muertos

Serves 12

- 1/3 cup water
- 4½ tablespoons butter
- 4½ eggs
- ½ cup sugar
- ¾ teaspoon salt
- 1/3 teaspoon orange zest
- 1/8 teaspoon star anise
- 2 1/3 cups bread flour
- 1½ teaspoons bread machine yeast

1. Whisk together the dry ingredients and set aside.
2. Add the liquid ingredients to the bread maker pan first, then gently pour the mixed dry ingredients on top of the liquid.
3. Set for Sweet cycle, medium crust color, and press Start.
4. Transfer to a cooling rack for 20 minutes before slicing to serve.

Sweet Mexican Bread

Serves 12

- 1 cup whole milk
- ¼ cup butter
- 1 egg
- ¼ cup sugar
- 1 teaspoon salt
- 3 cups bread flour
- 1½ teaspoons yeast

1. Add wet ingredients to bread maker pan.
2. Add dry ingredients, except yeast.
3. Make a well in the center of the dry ingredients and add the yeast.
4. Set to Sweet cycle, light crust color, and press Start.
5. Remove to a cooling rack for 15 minutes before serving.

Authentic Challah

Serves 12

- ½ cup warm water
- 1 package active dry yeast
- 1 tablespoon sugar
- 3 tablespoons butter, softened
- ½ teaspoon kosher salt
- 2 to 2½ cups kosher all-purpose flour
- 2 eggs
- 1 egg yolk
- 1 teaspoon water

1. Add sugar and salt to bread maker pan.
2. Add butter, eggs, then water.
3. Add flour and yeast.
4. Select Dough cycle and press Start.
5. Transfer dough to a large mixing bowl sprayed with non-stick cooking spray. Spray dough with non-stick cooking spray and cover. Let rise in a warm place until doubled in size; about 45 minutes.
6. Punch dough down. Remove dough to lightly floured surface; pat dough and shape into a 10-by-6-inch rectangle.
7. Divide into 3 equal strips with a pizza cutter. Braid strips and place into a 9-by-5-inch loaf pan sprayed with non-stick cooking spray. Cover and let rise in warm place for about 30 to 45 minutes.
8. Beat egg yolk with 1 teaspoon water and baste loaf.
9. Bake at 375ºF (190ºC) for 25 to 30 minutes, or until golden.
10. Let cool on a rack for 5 minutes before removing from loaf pan and serve.

Russian Caraway and Fennel Rye Bread

Serves 1

- 1¼ cups dark rye flour
- 2½ cups unbleached flour
- 1 teaspoon instant coffee
- 2 tablespoons unsweetened cocoa powder
- 1 tablespoon whole caraway seeds
- ½ teaspoon dried minced onion
- ½ teaspoon fennel seeds
- 1 teaspoon sea salt
- 2 teaspoons active dry yeast
- 1⅓ cups water, at room temperature
- 1 teaspoon sugar
- 1½ tablespoons dark molasses
- 1½ tablespoons apple cider vinegar
- 3 tablespoons vegetable oil

1. Mix dry ingredients together in a bowl, except for yeast.
2. Add wet ingredients to bread pan first; top with dry ingredients.
3. Make a well in the center of the dry ingredients and add the yeast.
4. Select Basic cycle, medium crust color, and press Start.
5. Let cool for 15 minutes before slicing.

Russian Coriander and Caraway Rye Bread

Serves 12

- 1¼ cups warm water
- 1¾ cups rye flour
- 1¾ cups whole wheat flour
- 2 tablespoons malt (or beer kit mixture)
- 1 tablespoon molasses
- 2 tablespoons white vinegar
- 1 teaspoon salt
- ½ tablespoon coriander seeds
- ½ tablespoon caraway seeds
- 2 teaspoons active dry yeast

1. Mix dry ingredients together in a bowl, except for yeast.
2. Add wet ingredients to bread pan first; top with dry ingredients.
3. Make a well in the center of the dry ingredients and add the yeast.
4. Press Basic cycle, choose medium crust color, and press Start.
5. Remove from bread pan and allow to cool on a wire rack before serving.

Hawaiian Pineapple Bread

Serves 12

- ¾ cup pineapple juice
- 1 egg
- 2 tablespoons olive oil
- 2 tablespoons whole milk
- 2½ tablespoons sugar
- ¾ teaspoon salt
- 3 cups bread flour
- 1½ teaspoons active dry yeast

1. Add the wet ingredients to bread maker pan, then add sugar, salt and flour.
2. Make a well in the center of the dry ingredients and add the yeast
3. Press Basic cycle, choose medium crust color, and press Start.
4. Remove from bread pan and allow to cool before serving.

Easter Bread

Serves 12

- ⅔ cup fresh butter
- 1 cup milk
- 1 cup sugar
- 1 teaspoon mastic
- ½ teaspoon salt
- 1 package active dry yeast
- 3 eggs
- 5 cups strong yellow flour
- 1 egg, for brushing blended with 1 teaspoon water

1. Heat milk and butter until melted in a saucepan; do not boil. Add to bread maker pan.
2. Add sugar and mastic to a food processor and blend; add to bread maker pan.
3. Add remaining ingredients.
4. Set Dough cycle and press Start; leave dough to rise one hour after cycle.
5. Shape into 2 loaves, cover, and leave to rise for 50 more minutes.
6. Baste with egg wash.
7. Bake at 320ºF (160ºC) for 30 to 40 minutes or until golden brown.
8. Transfer to cooling rack for 15 minutes before serving.

British Cinnamon Raisin Hot Cross Buns

Serves 12

- ¾ cup warm milk
- 3 tablespoons butter, unsalted
- ¼ cup white sugar
- ½ teaspoon salt
- 1 egg

For Brushing:
- 1 egg yolk

For the Crosses:
- 2 tablespoons flour
- Cold water

- 1 egg white
- 3 cups all-purpose flour
- 1 tablespoon active dry yeast
- ¾ cup dried raisins
- 1 teaspoon ground cinnamon

- 2 tablespoons water

- ½ tablespoon sugar

1. Put milk, butter, ¼ cup sugar, salt, egg, egg white, flour, and yeast in bread maker and start the Dough cycle.
2. Add raisins and cinnamon 5 minutes before kneading cycle ends.
3. Allow to rest in machine until doubled, about 30 minutes.
4. Punch down on a floured surface, cover, and let rest 10 minutes.
5. Shape into 12 balls and place in a greased 9-by-12-inch pan.
6. Cover and let rise in a warm place until doubled, about 35-40 minutes.
7. Mix egg yolk and 2 tablespoons water and baste each bun.
8. Mix the cross ingredients to form pastry.
9. Roll out pastry and cut into thin strips. Place across the buns to form crosses.
10. Bake at 375ºF (190ºC) for 20 minutes.
11. Remove from pan immediately and cool on a rack. Serve warm.

Za'atar Bread

Serves 12 to 14

- ⅓ cup za'atar seasoning
- 2 tablespoons onion powder
- 1 cup warm water
- 2 tablespoons agave nectar

- ¼ cup applesauce
- 3 cups bread flour
- 1 teaspoon salt
- 2¼ teaspoons rapid rise yeast

1. Mix dry ingredients together in a bowl, except for yeast.
2. Add wet ingredients to bread pan first; top with dry ingredients.
3. Make a well in the center of the dry ingredients and add the yeast.
4. Press Basic cycle, choose medium crust color, and press Start.
5. Remove from bread pan and allow to cool before serving.

Portuguese Cornmeal Bread

Serves 8

- 1 cup yellow cornmeal
- 1¼ cups cold water, divided
- 1½ teaspoons active dry yeast
- 1½ cups bread flour
- 2 teaspoons sugar
- ¾ teaspoon salt
- 1 tablespoon olive oil

1. Stir cornmeal into ¾ cup of the cold water until lumps disappear.
2. Add cornmeal mixture and oil to bread maker pan.
3. Add remaining dry ingredients, except yeast, to pan.
4. Make a well in the center of the dry ingredients and add the yeast.
5. Choose Sweet cycle, light crust color and press Start.
6. Transfer to plate and serve warm.

Panettone

Serves 16

- ¾ cup warm water
- 4 large egg yolks
- 2 teaspoons vanilla extract
- ½ cup sugar
- 1 teaspoon lemon zest
- 1 teaspoon orange zest
- ½ teaspoon salt
- ½ cup unsalted butter, softened and cut into pieces
- 3¼ cups unbleached flour
- 1 package bread machine yeast
- ½ cup golden raisins
- ½ cup raisins
- 1 egg white, slightly beaten
- 4 sugar cubes, crushed

1. Add the water, egg yolks, vanilla, and zest to the bread maker pan.
2. Add the sugar, salt, and flour.
3. Lay pieces of butter around the outside of the pan on top of the flour.
4. Press a well into the flour and add the yeast.
5. Start the Dough cycle; at the second kneading cycle add golden raisins and raisins.
6. Let dough rise until doubled.
7. Prepare the pan/baking case: cut a circle of parchment paper to line the bottom of the 6-inch cake pan and spray with non-stick cooking spray.
8. Cut another piece of parchment to line the inside of the brown paper bag after you have cut the bottom out of the bag.
9. Fold the top edge down to form a cuff then spray the inside of the parchment with cooking spray. Place the paper case in the pan.

10. Punch the dough down and knead into a ball.
11. Add it to the paper-lined pan case and allow to rise until almost doubled.
12. Preheat the oven to 350ºF (180ºC).
13. Baste the top of the panettone dough with the beaten egg white and sprinkle with the crushed sugar cubes.
14. Bake for 30 minutes, then reduce heat to 325ºF (163ºC) and bake another 30 minutes.
15. Remove from oven and allow to cool in pan for about 15 minutes, then cool on a rack until ready to serve.

Simple Amish Bread

Serves 12

- 1⅛ cups warm water
- 1 package active dry yeast
- 2¾ cups wheat flour
- ½ teaspoon salt
- ⅓ cup sugar
- ¼ cup canola oil
- 1 large egg

1. Add warm water, sugar and yeast to bread maker pan; let sit for 8 minutes or until it foams.
2. Add remaining ingredients to the pan.
3. Select Basic cycle, light crust color, and press Start.
4. Transfer to a cooling rack for 20 minutes before slicing.

Fiji Sweet Potato Bread

Serves 12

- 1¼ cups sweet potato, mashed
- 10 tablespoons canned coconut milk
- 1 teaspoon ginger, fresh grated
- 1 tablespoon lemon zest
- 2 tablespoons honey
- 2 tablespoons olive oil
- 3 cups bread flour
- 1 teaspoon salt
- 2¼ teaspoons rapid rise yeast

1. Add the wet ingredients to bread maker pan.
2. Mix dry ingredients, except for yeast, in a bowl. Add to pan.
3. Make a well in the center of the dry ingredients and add the yeast.
4. Press Basic cycle, choose medium crust color, and press Start.
5. Remove from bread pan and allow to cool before serving.

Appendix 1 Measurement Conversion Chart

VOLUME EQUIVALENTS(DRY)

US STANDARD	METRIC (APPROXIMATE)
1/8 teaspoon	0.5 mL
1/4 teaspoon	1 mL
1/2 teaspoon	2 mL
3/4 teaspoon	4 mL
1 teaspoon	5 mL
1 tablespoon	15 mL
1/4 cup	59 mL
1/2 cup	118 mL
3/4 cup	177 mL
1 cup	235 mL
2 cups	475 mL
3 cups	700 mL
4 cups	1 L

VOLUME EQUIVALENTS(LIQUID)

US STANDARD	US STANDARD (OUNCES)	METRIC (APPROXIMATE)
2 tablespoons	1 fl.oz.	30 mL
1/4 cup	2 fl.oz.	60 mL
1/2 cup	4 fl.oz.	120 mL
1 cup	8 fl.oz.	240 mL
1 1/2 cup	12 fl.oz.	355 mL
2 cups or 1 pint	16 fl.oz.	475 mL
4 cups or 1 quart	32 fl.oz.	1 L
1 gallon	128 fl.oz.	4 L

TEMPERATURES EQUIVALENTS

FAHRENHEIT(F)	CELSIUS(C) (APPROXIMATE)
225 °F	107 °C
250 °F	120 °C
275 °F	135 °C
300 °F	150 °C
325 °F	160 °C
350 °F	180 °C
375 °F	190 °C
400 °F	205 °C
425 °F	220 °C
450 °F	235 °C
475 °F	245 °C
500 °F	260 °C

WEIGHT EQUIVALENTS

US STANDARD	METRIC (APPROXIMATE)
1 ounce	28 g
2 ounces	57 g
5 ounces	142 g
10 ounces	284 g
15 ounces	425 g
16 ounces (1 pound)	455 g
1.5 pounds	680 g
2 pounds	907 g

Appendix 2 Recipe Index

A
Almond Milk Bread 55
Almond-Coconut Pumpkin Bread 78
Apple Bread 27
Authentic Challah 83

B
Baisc Whole-Wheat Sourdough Bread 63
Balsamic and Sour Cream Rye Bread 15
Balsamic Onion Rye Bread 29
Banana Bread with Walnut 27
Banana-Chocolate Oat Bread 54
Barmbrack 51
Basic Whole Wheat Bread 11
Beer Rye Whole Wheat Bread 17
Beer Sourdough Bread 66
Black Pepper White Bread 39
British Cinnamon Raisin Hot Cross Buns 86
Buttermilk Lavender Bread 37
Buttermilk Nutmeat Bread 72
Buttermilk Spelt Bread 14

C-D
Cajun Bread 38
Candied-Ginger Oat Bread 43
Caraway Rye Bread 17
Cardamom and Turmeric Bread 37
Cardamom Bread 42
Cheddar Cheese Sourdough Oat Bread 67
Chive and Parsley Pull-Apart Rolls 29
Chocolate Sourdough Bread wtih Pistachios 69
Cinnamon Butter Rolls 47
Cinnamon Date Walnut Swirl Bread 32
Cinnamon Prune Whole Wheat Bread 26
Cinnamon White Bread 40
Citrus Sourdough Egg Bread 65
Classic Italian Cornmeal Bread 82
Coconut Bread 76
Coconut Pumpkin Bread 56
Coffee Cake with Pecans 53
Coffee Dark Bread 51
Cracked Rye Sesame Bread 20
Cream Cheese Dill Bread 35
Crystallized Ginger Carrot Bread 26
Dutch Dark Rye Bread 16

E-F
Easter Bread 85
Easy Herb and Garlic Cream Cheese Bread 40
Faux Apple Cider Sourdough Bread 64
Fiji Sweet Potato Bread 88

G
Garden Herb Bread 36
Garlic Bread 41
Garlic Butter Bread 23
Granola Bread 53
Greek Sour Cream Chocolate Bread 57

H
Hawaiian Pineapple Bread 85
Hazelnut Bread 76
Herb and Walnut Bread 28
Herb Bread 35
Herb Swirl Semolina Bread 45
Herbed Parmesan Pesto Bread 41
Herbed Sourdough Bread 68
Honey Apple Butter Bread 52
Honey Black Olive Rye Bread 23
Honey Bread 56

Honey Flaxseed Bread 74
Honey Sourdough Bread 67
Honey-Lemon Anise Bread 42

L

Lemony Rosemary Hazelnut Bread 44
Limpa Bread 18
Lush Herb Hazelnut Bread 38
Lush Seed and Oat Bread 78

M-N

Maple Whole Wheat White Bread 15
Milk Sourdough Bread 65
Mint Chocolate Bread 43
Monkey Bread with Raisins 59
Multigrain Cereal Sourdough Bread 64
Nectarine Bread 50
No-Yeast Sourdough Starter 69
No-Yeast Whole-Wheat Sourdough Starter 62
Nut and Seed Bread 75

O

Oat and Sunflower Seed Bread 72
Orange Rye Bread 16

P

Pan de Muertos 82
Panettone 87
Parsley Corn Bread 28
Peanut Butter-Chocolate Banana Bread 57
Pecan Bread 74
Pecan-Cranberry Sourdough Bread 62
Pine Nut Basil Bread 46
Polish Chocolate Bread 58
Portuguese Cornmeal Bread 87
Prosciutto Bread 30
Pumpernickel Bread 18
Pumpkin Paximadia 19
Pure Whole Wheat Bread 13

R

Raisin Breadsticks 46
Ranch Wheat Bran Whole Wheat Bread 14
Russian Caraway and Fennel Rye Bread 84
Russian Coriander and Caraway Rye Bread 84
Rye Seed Bread 77

S

Sesame and Chia Seed Bread 77
Sesame and FlaxSeed Bread with Raisins 79
Simple Amish Bread 88
Skim Milk Sourdough Bread 66
Sour Cream Bread 50
Sourdough Bread 63
Sourdough Starter 68
Spiced Honey Egg Bread 39
Sun-Dried Tomato Whole Wheat Bread 24
Sunflower and Sesame Seed Bread 73
Super Seed Whole Wheat Bread 13
Sweet Apple Bread 55
Sweet Mexican Bread 83
Sweet Potato Bread with Cranberry 24

T-V

Toasted Sesame Seed Whole Wheat Bread 12
Triple Seed Bread 75
Vanilla Peanut Butter Bread 52
Walnut Bread 73

W

Wheat Berry Bread with Cherries 25
Whole Wheat Honey Bread 11
Whole Wheat Sesame Bread 12
Wildflower Honey Herb Bread 36
Winter Squash Cloverleaf Rolls 31

Z

Za'atar Bread 86
Zucchini Whole Wheat Bread 25

www.ingramcontent.com/pod-product-compliance
Ingram Content Group UK Ltd.
Pitfield, Milton Keynes, MK11 3LW, UK
UKHW050830020925
7661UKWH00033B/16